What you need to know about my past is that no matter what has happened, it has all worked together to bring me to this very moment and this is the moment I can choose to make everything new— right now.

PICTURED FROM LEFT TO RIGHT: MY OLDEST DAUGHTER, STACIE CLARK; MY OLDEST GRANDSON, LAKE CLARK; MY SON, BART YATES; ME, SYLVIA YATES; MY GRANDDAUGHTER, SAYLOR CLARK; MY YOUNGEST GRANDSON, BRYLAN YATES; MY YOUNGEST DAUGHTER, KACIE YATES.

Dedicated with love to my three children, who never gave up on me, and to my three grandchildren, who helped make my life whole again.

SYLVIA

CONTENTS

INTRODUCTION

I'm Sylvia, and I'm an addict. I wish it weren't true, but it is. I tried to hide the terrible truth for 17 years, but those six simple words carry a story of embarrassment and disgrace that will haunt me the rest of my life. They acknowledge publicly the torment I lived in—and the torture I put my family through—for far too many years.

Those same words—with different names—are quietly uttered by every addict who attends a Narcotics Anonymous (NA) meeting as we go around the circle, introducing ourselves. The first time I said them aloud it sounded like a stranger speaking. I couldn't believe I was saying, "I am an addict." Actually, I had said the words before—when I had been through treatment twice previously—but I hadn't meant them because I didn't believe them. I had long denied my addiction, pretending I could stop taking the pills whenever I wanted. I had looked at my family and lied about why I was so lethargic, why I didn't want to do anything or go anywhere, why I kept losing job after job. I tried to convince them—and myself—that I was okay.

But reality finally found its way into my drug-distorted mind. When I said, "I am an addict" this time, I believed it. Declaring aloud what I knew in my heart to be true was intensely painful, but it was the first step to recovery and I knew it had to be taken. I thought I had hit rock bottom before, but this time I had crashed so hard I didn't know if I could ever get up. To have any hope of climbing out of the chasm into which I had fallen, I had to come clean, especially to myself.

I'm Sherry, and I'm here to support Sylvia. As I say the words, I know they are just part of the story. I am at the NA meeting to support my sister, but the truth is that I am not just one of her supporters; I am an enabler. For more than a decade, I sent money to her when she called, desperate for funds. Even when I suspected she was using the money to buy pills, I couldn't say no. And, when she was in trouble, I repeatedly bailed her out because I couldn't bear watching her face the consequences of her actions. I thought I was helping, but the unvarnished truth is, I was doing more harm than good by helping hide her drug habit and enabling her to remain a slave to addiction.

ʃ

How can it be that Sylvia is an addict? We're just average, middle-class people—not movie stars who make headlines when their addiction becomes public or thugs who grew up in the underworld of drugs. Beautiful, lithe Sylvia: cheerleader, homecoming queen, captain of her basketball team in high school. Played ball in college but majored in handsome men; married one and had three gorgeous children. Lived in beautiful homes; played tennis competitively. Dressed exquisitely. Now, all of that is history. So much has been lost through her powerlessness to addiction. So much damage has been done to her shattered family.

We—Sylvia and Sherry—sisters by blood and friends by choice—wrote this book to reveal how an average person can be caught in the far-reaching and unrelenting tentacles of substance abuse. To put faces behind the words, "I'm ___ and I'm an addict." To illustrate the injuries inflicted on the victim and the family by addiction. To share Sylvia's story and others like hers so you will know you are not alone—that you're not so different after all—if you are an addict or have an addict in your family.

Addiction is ugly and it's not curable. But it doesn't have to be fatal—for the addict or the family. Many addicts survive to live a better life, and broken families are often healed. But admitting the condition, acknowledging the awful reality, requires courage. And staying clean takes commitment and determination. The temptation to abuse again is always there. But the power to fight—and even begin the battle anew—lies within, sometimes just beneath the surface and sometimes buried so deeply it seems impossible to find. The trick is to unearth it before it is too late.

Running throughout this book is Sylvia's story—how she became hooked on drugs, how she first fought to hang on to them and then struggled to break the tenacious hold they had on her, and how she has finally found hope and peace. But it is much more than that; HOOKED BUT NOT HOPELESS paints a picture of addiction and the addict, shedding light on the causes and effects of the disease. It takes the reader to a cavity in the drug culture where even "average" people—our family, friends, and neighbors—fall and can't climb out. It provides insight for families who must deal with the addiction of someone dearly loved. Families who suffer alongside the addict, who live through his or her disappointments and troubles, who never lose hope and rejoice when recovery comes.

Reading Sylvia's story—and those of other addicts whose lives are shared in the book—will help victims and their families understand the disease of addiction, and in doing so, enable them to comprehend how "normal" people can lose control of their lives. How the hook looks so inviting yet causes so much pain. How the journey through the river of addiction is fraught with white water and treacherous falls. But most of all, hope that the hook can be dislodged and cast aside—how recovery is possible.

AUTHORS' NOTE: *This book is primarily about prescription drug addiction, but because of the similarities with alcohol abuse, that topic is also included. Other than brief references in personal stories, other types of abuse are not addressed. Even so, many of the principles, causes, and habits are similar, regardless of the substance of choice.*

PART ONE

*Understanding the Addict and the Disease
Through a Close-Up Lens*

CHAPTER 1

THE BEGINNING OF THE END

Sylvia

September 1989. I don't remember the exact date, the weather, or the trees that were undoubtedly vibrant in their fall splendor, but the event resulting in my taking the first Lortab (hydrocodone) pill will be etched in my mind forever. I'll never forget how it made me feel—a miracle drug that took away the pain of my husband cheating and making me feel like I deserved it. And I'll never fail to remember it was the beginning of an extended nightmare for me and for my family.

I wish there was some way to go back and change things, but I would have to return so far, beginning with that first pill; and time moves only forward. If I had just known all the horrible events that would result from that one little pill, I would have never taken it. I wonder what my life would have been today. Would I still be married to Don? Would we be happy? If I could only go back....

Don and I were married for 21 years, and like most couples, we experienced good times and bad ones. On balance, we had an enjoyable life—supporting our three children in sports, taking them to church, and trying to provide a healthy home environment. But, it wasn't all peaches and cream; our marriage had a hidden darkness I didn't see for a long time.

When my husband Don left home after a heated argument and didn't come home for several weeks, I suspected he was having an affair. Even though he convincingly denied cheating on me, our kids and I knew something was going on. In the months before he left us, he rarely came home from *work until 11 p.m. or later. When he did arrive before dark, sometimes he would just stand in the back yard and somberly stare into space. I could tell he didn't see the mountain range towering in the distance. He didn't even reach down and pet E.T., our boxer, who seemed to sense Don's sadness. And he didn't pay much attention to the kids any more, showing up at their ballgames late and ignoring them when they ran down the driveway crying after him when he would come home for a few hours and then leave.*

I never knew if Don was living with his girlfriend or with his parents, but after a couple of months away from home, he moved back in with us. He was still acting strangely, as if he were in a different world. I think he was struggling with whether to leave or stay, and to calm his conscience, he picked fights with me. The more we argued, the more violent he became. And the more aggressive he was, the less I desired him, and that made him increasingly brutal. One morning, in the heat of anger, he picked up a radio and lobbed it at me like a basketball. Out of control, he pulled me by my hair and hurled me on the bed, beating my face with his fists as he screamed, "Yeah, I f***ing have somebody and they still want me, and I'm going to blow your f***ing brains out." When Don ran downstairs, my gut shouted to me, "He's going to grab his gun!" Terrified, I slipped down the back stairs and ran to the horse barn, still in my pajamas. (Don denies this happened to this day. If he admitted anything happened at all, I'm sure he would say he was only trying to scare me.)

I'm not sure why he didn't look for me in the barn, but I know if he had, he would have killed me because he was so enraged. Instead, he stayed in the house for about 30 minutes and then, as I cowered in the barn, watching fearfully through a crack in the door, I saw him leave. I waited until I was sure he wasn't going to return and then slipped back into the house. My head hurting where Don had hit me, I knew I needed to see a doctor. Distraught and in pain, I didn't think I could drive myself, so I called a friend, and she came to take me. Thankfully, the X-rays didn't show a concussion or any broken bones—just bad bruises on my face and arms. The doctor advised me to call the police, but I didn't—afraid it would make Don even madder and bring embarrassment to our kids. Looking back, I guess I was just plain humiliated—I didn't want anyone to know I was married to a man who abused me.

My friend Anna and I rode around a while after we left the doctor's office, scared Don had returned to our house and was waiting for me. As we talked, I tried to make it seem not as bad as it was, but Anna could see through my pretense. It wasn't easy to hide how troubled I was, especially the depth of my depression from the emotional badgering that was more damaging than the physical abuse. When Anna finally took me home, we checked to make sure Don's car wasn't in the driveway or garage before I got out. Concerned about leaving me in such a state of distress, before she left, Anna offered me a pain pill saying, "Here, Sylvia. Take this. It will help your headache and might even cheer you up." Such a tiny little thing, but it was the beginning of an agonizing journey that wouldn't end for 17 years.

As I later learned is typical of abusive spouses, when Don came home that night, he told me how sorry he was and that he would never do it again. As usual, he tried to make me feel it was my fault—and he succeeded.

Don was a master at shifting responsibility. I always defended him when talking with counselors, telling them he only hit me on a few occasions. Each time, the counselor looked at me like I was irrational—even crazy— assuring me that no matter what I did or didn't do, he had no right to hit me—even one time. I had a hard time accepting the counselors' assertions that any man who hit a woman was an abusive husband. I just didn't want to believe that about the father of my children, so I tried to take some of the guilt from him by blaming myself. Even today, I have a hard time convincing myself all of our problems weren't my fault. Don would say, "I've talked to a lot of men, and they all said they didn't blame me—they would have affairs, too, if their wives were cold to them." I realize now it was wrong for me not to give the affection he demanded, but at the time, it was the only way I knew to deal with how he was acting. Don just didn't understand that because of his cheating and other problems I had lost all desire for him.

I know deep inside me that the issues in my marriage with Don arose because of his multiple, ongoing affairs and abuse, which resulted in my bitterness toward him, but he was good at controlling how I thought, making me feel guilty. He still is....

That day, I decided I would never let him hurt me again. I would get a job and file for a divorce, just as my counselor had advised. But we still lived together for several more months, and to survive, I started to take pain pills like the one Anna had given me more frequently. They were easy to get—her brother was a dentist, and he didn't hesitate to write me prescriptions, just as he did for Anna. At first, I took three or so hydrocodones a week. Then five or six a week. Then one or two a day and then more and more. I felt better emotionally than I had in a long time. The pills gave me confidence and self-esteem, feelings Don had taken away from me through repeated emotional abuse. I was so bitter I knew I could never forgive him.

Lulled into complacency by the pills, I tried to convince myself I didn't care if my husband had had affairs for the past 21 years. I didn't care that he was having one now. All I wanted to do was show him I was worth something—that someone else might appreciate me since he made me feel he didn't. Even though he told me he loved me, it was hard to believe him because of the way he treated me. I was hurting so badly, I had soon unwittingly committed myself to have my own affair. The biggest mistake I ever made was not turning my hurt and pain over to God instead of trying to handle it myself. But I had made up my mind to leave Don, and I needed something more than pain pills to give me the courage to carry out my plan to hurt Don the way he had hurt me. I needed to drive away the anxiety and beat down my conscience about what I knew was wrong.

I went to a psychiatrist who prescribed Zanax (alapralozam)—he was glad to give me all I wanted. With both Zanax and hydrocodones, I felt I had everything under control. I let myself be seduced by a good-looking, sweet-talking man I met where I worked. He made me feel good about myself, and he treated me like I had always wanted to be treated. I thought Bill was everything Don wasn't—a successful businessman who treated me like a queen.

But then disaster struck. Don found out about Bill. Furious, he showed up at Bill's house and fired his pistol through the front window. Then, larger and physically stronger than Bill, he dragged Bill outside and beat him, breaking several ribs. When I saw what he was doing to Bill, I ran outside. Don thought I was trying to protect Bill, but the truth was I was trying to save Don from going to jail for killing someone. Don didn't believe that—he beat me up and then took his belt off and thrashed me in the head with the buckle. Suddenly, my life was splashed across local television screens and newspapers. My kids were mortified, and I was made to look like a cheating wife while Don played the role of the innocent one, even though he had been cheating for years. Now, he managed to make himself look like the victim. It just wasn't fair.

The wonderful man who I thought was going to be my escape route from an abusive marriage was not so wonderful. Although he never beat me, he did knock me down once, and he damaged me emotionally as I was forced to deal with his mental instability. Later, I discovered he had a pattern of preying on women who weren't happy with their husbands or were needy in some way. Even after I realized the guy was half crazy, I still clung to him, afraid of being alone. I had never lived by myself or been responsible for a home or anything else. I married Don while I was in college, and we had been together for 21 years—I was scared to death of being on my own.

To deal with my fear, I took more and more pills. Soon, with my divorce final, I was alone to deal with finding a place for my kids and me to *live, to be sure we had food on the table, to support the kids in school and other activities. The court had awarded me a small part of the money from the sale of our home, but much of that was used to purchase pills and to buy my kids clothes and other items to make up for the pain I had caused them. Money was a constant problem because Don was erratic about paying alimony and child support. Some months he didn't pay me at all, and at other times, he only gave me part of the court-ordered payment. Faced with regular bills and no steady income, I became frantic. Although I tried to handle it, I couldn't face life without pills.*

Within a month of the divorce, Don married again. I downed more pills to deal with that. Six months later, Don divorced. While we were trying to put our marriage back together (at least I thought we were), Don started dating one of my so-called friends. Soon they were married, and I knew my aloneness was permanent. I felt lost and abandoned. I blamed myself for breaking up our home, for tearing apart our family. Sometimes I think I would have grieved less if Don had died. Instead, I had to see him at my kids' ballgames and other places with a new wife. Even now, after so many years, I berate myself that I could have saved my marriage and my family if I had acted differently. I know that sounds crazy, but Don had convinced me he was a good husband and I was the one who filed for the divorce for no reason.

When the hurt was so raw at the beginning, it was more than I could bear without massive numbers of Zanax and hydrocodones. But the more pills I took to fight my depression and anxiety, the more frightened and despondent I became. They numbed me, and that kept me from learning to deal with my changed life.

To combat the ongoing guilt, sadness, and depression, I popped pills. I didn't know it, but I had become a drug addict. I was hooked.

Addiction doesn't just affect the addict; it touches everyone close by, shaking the foundation of a family and leaving heart-rending stains that are hard to erase, even after recovery. In Sylvia's family, her youngest daughter Kacie took the brunt of the burden of her mother's abuse because she was so young. The precocious, blond-haired beauty found her happy life turned into a nightmare as she watched her mom descend into the abyss of addiction.

Kacie

I first realized my mom was addicted to prescription drugs when I was a sophomore in high school. I probably suspected she was taking pills earlier than that but didn't realize it was a problem until I was 16. I knew something was wrong because she went from being the person I looked up to the most in the world, the person I knew I could depend on for anything, to being someone I didn't know, recognize, or get along with. I knew she wasn't the mother I had always known when no matter how upset I got or how hard I cried while pleading with her to just be honest with me about taking pills, nothing would shake her. She was completely numb to me and that wasn't my mom.

I "officially" found out that she was abusing pain killers the night she stole milk and pop tarts from Walmart. The Sylvia Yates I had loved since birth was full of honesty, class, and dignity. In the past, she would have prayed for someone who stole groceries or anything else.

My sister Stacie and I picked her up that night, and I remember thinking that would be her wakeup call. Little did I know her wakeup call wouldn't come for 12 more years.

Stacie

I first suspected Mom was taking too many pills when her eyes could barely stay open even when I was talking to her. She never seemed to feel well and was tired all of the time, and that wasn't like her. Still, when she got caught stealing the milk and pop tarts, I was shocked. When the security guard told Kacie and me that our mother had a serious problem, I didn't want to admit it; but after that night I knew I had no choice—my mom was an addict and something needed to be done to help her.

Bart

I had been out of high school for about a year when my mom and dad divorced, and I went back and forth, sometimes living with her and sometimes living with him. So, I wasn't around as much as Kacie and Stacie, but I was there enough to know something was wrong. Like Stacie, when we were living in Hamilton Mill, I remember mom would fall asleep while I was talking to her—she would be sitting up, but her eyes would start drooping and then they would close altogether. At that point, I knew she was taking too much medication, but I had no idea she was addicted.

WHO GETS HOOKED?

Who is a drug addict? Narcotics Anonymous gives a simple answer: "Very simply, an addict is a man or woman whose life is controlled by drugs." Many believe the disease begins long before the first time a person uses a mind-altering substance—that some people are predisposed to addiction. Why can one individual have a drink or two and not crave more while another can't stop until the bottle is empty? Why can one person take narcotics following surgery and then stop when pain diminishes, while someone else gets hooked? What makes some people cross the line from occasional medicinal or social use to full-blown addiction?

Are some people simply stronger than others, able to resist the temptation for more of a particular substance that gives them feelings of pleasure or relief? Myriad research projects suggest that to attribute the cause of addiction to such a character flaw is shortsighted and far less complicated than the disease requires. While addiction may be influenced by personality and environment, the beginnings of the disease may be in genes. Just as cancer can lurk in blood cells for years before symptoms appear, addiction may have neurobiological or chemical roots that lie in wait for the first drink or the first pill to release their out-of-control cravings through the body.

WHY DOES A PERSON TAKE THE BAIT?

The purpose of this book does not allow for an exhaustive report on current research studies, but the following brief summaries of some work over the past decade suggest addiction is not a choice—it is a chemical reaction over which the person has no control after the first drink or pill is taken. Abuse causes changes in the brain that affect thinking, making it difficult for addicts to think rationally.

The changes start with serotonin and dopamine, chemicals in the brain that carry messages to neurons, specialized cells whose job is to process and transmit information. Although both serotonin and dopamine are neurotransmitters, they affect the brain in different ways.

Animal studies have demonstrated that levels of serotonin are lower in the brains of addicts than non-addicts and that the level of dopamine increases when alcohol or drugs are ingested. In simplest terms, when levels of serotonin are lowered, the ability of humans to focus and make connections with other parts of the brain is lessened. At lower levels, tolerance thresholds decline, and a person can be propelled to action in an instant, seeking safety or satisfaction.

Ruden and Byalick (2003) describe dopamine as the "gotta have it" and serotonin as the "got it." If the level of serotonin is low, the person doesn't feel he or she "has it" [safety, comfort, pleasure, etc.]. If the lowered level of serotonin is combined with rising levels of dopamine caused by drugs or alcohol, the person loses control—"gotta have it" takes control over the mind and pushes the person to do whatever it takes to "get" what he or she needs.

Another study, advanced as a breakthrough by scientists at the University of Cambridge in 2007, focused on changes in a neurotransmitter receptor in a particular part of the brain. Using positron emission tomography (a PET scan), the researchers demonstrated that rats who were behaviorally impulsive, even without exposure to drugs, had significantly less brain dopamine receptors than their more restrained counterparts. Additionally, these same impulsive rats were more likely to self-administer cocaine intravenously, thus linking addiction vulnerability to impulsive behavior. This research is important because it demonstrates that the alterations in dopamine receptors and impulsivity pre-date drug use rather than emerging as a result of prolonged addiction. In other words, the brains of addicts may be genetically engineered differently than the brains of those who can drink responsibly and who can take drugs without becoming addicted. Addiction, according to this theory, is a compulsive brain disorder. If researchers can identify the gene or genes that cause[s] the diminished supply of brain receptors, treatment therapies could be dramatically affected.

Other research, as reported by Colvin in his 2008 book, has shown that, "after prolonged use of an addictive substance, the 'circuits' in the brain become, in effect, 'rewired.'" He describes this alteration: "When a medication enters the brain, it is absorbed through receptor sites. Addictive drugs are believed to act on the brain by reinforcing the action of the brain's natural chemical, dopamine, [which] is involved in producing the sensation of pleasure. When the body is getting such chemicals from an outside source, the body stops making some of its own and becomes dependent on the outside source. As the brain adapts to the drug's presence, the individual using the drugs develops tolerance and must continually increase the dosage in order to maintain the initial pleasure sensations."

Colvin adds that the individual may intellectually understand the destructive consequences of addiction but cannot stop the compulsive use of a drug, because the changes in brain structure have affected emotions and motivation, both of which affect behavior.

ESCAPING FROM THE HOOK IS NOT EASY

While research on physical causes is still evolving, one fact is clear: Addicts do not choose to become addicted. And they can't "just quit." It is not a matter of willpower. It is more related to the genetic and chemical makeup of a person than to an individual's desire to escape from the hook.

Other factors also contribute to continued addiction. The most frequently reported reasons for not receiving treatment include (1) not ready to stop using; (2) no health insurance and costs are prohibitive; (3) potential negative impact on job or image; (4) belief that the problem can be handled without treatment; and (5) not knowing where to find treatment.

Addressing these issues requires desire and commitment. Addiction is a disease that must be diagnosed and treated, just like tenacious cancers. In the same sense that some cancers are hard to detect and may not be curable, addiction is sometimes difficult to uncover and is incurable. But it is treatable. "Remission" is possible.

HOW MANY ARE HOOKED?

If addiction is hard to identify, how many addicts walk among us?

It is impossible to determine the number of people misusing drugs and alcohol, but what is certain is that the number has increased dramatically over the past decade. According to the National Survey on Drug Use and Health, in 2009 an estimated 21.8 million Americans aged 12 or older were current users, compared to 9.3 million in 1999. Today, almost 10 percent of the population abuse drugs such as marijuana/hashish, cocaine (including crack), heroin, hallucinogens, inhalants, or prescription-style psychotherapeutics.

Among the 10 percent abusing drugs are an alarming number of troops returning from Iraq or Afghanistan. A recent news article described the military medical system as "awash in prescription drugs." With more than 300,000 troops suffering from post-traumatic stress disorder, depression, traumatic brain injury, or some combination of those, military psychiatrists are prescribing more drugs—both narcotic painkillers and anti-anxiety/anti-depressant medications. When troops are treated with both, the tranquilizing effects amplify, and the powerful drug cocktails cause drug dependency, suicide, and fatal accidents. And, it's affecting troops in combat as well as those who have returned home.

Drug Abuse

Although addiction affects people in all walks of life, race/ethnicity, gender, age, and education appear to be factors in illicit drug use:

- College graduates are more likely to have tried illicit drugs than non-high school graduates (51.8% compared to 39.7%).

- Current drug use is lower for college graduates (6.1%) than for other groups: 9.8% for those with some college; 8.8% for high school graduates; 10.2% for high school dropouts.
- The highest rate of drug abuse is among American Indians and Alaska natives (18.3%), while the lowest rate is among Asians (3.7%).
- Illicit drug use is reported by 9.6% of Blacks, 8.8% of Caucasians, and 7.9% of Hispanics.
- Overall, males have a higher use rate (10.8%) than females (6.6%).

Alcohol Abuse

Alcohol abuse is also alarming. Slightly more than half of Americans aged 12 or older (approximately 130 million) drink alcohol, with 17.1 million reporting heavy drinking (defined as having five or more drinks on the same occasion on at least 5 days in the 30 days prior to the survey). Among young adults aged 18-25, the 2009 rate of binge drinking (defined as having five or more drinks on the same occasion on at least 1 day in the past 30 days) was 41.7 percent, compared to 8.8 percent for youth aged 12 to 17. Among older age groups, the prevalence of current alcohol use (heavy and binge drinking) decreased with increasing age, from 66.4 percent among 26- to 29-year-olds to 50.3 percent among 60- to 64-year-olds and 39.1 percent among people aged 65 or older.

In 2009, 12 percent of all Americans aged 12 or older admitted driving under the influence of alcohol at least once in the past year. In comparison, 4.2 percent drove while under the influence of drugs.

Alcohol use is higher among males (51.6 percent) than among females (46.5 percent). Whites are at the highest level (56.7 percent) among racial/ethnic users, with Blacks following at 42.8 percent and Hispanics at 41.7 percent. Asians drink at a higher level than they use drugs (37.6 percent), and Indians show the lowest level at 37.1 percent.

A View from the Micro Level

Diane Monteleone, Program Director of Focus Healthcare of Tennessee, reports that, until recently, 70 percent of patients at Focus were prescription drug addicts, 20 percent were addicted to street drugs, and 10 percent were addicted to polysubstances (three or more substances). Today, almost half are addicted to alcohol and half are addicted to opiates. This is related to a shift to older male and female patients, according to Monteleone.

What Substances Are Abused Most?

Overall, the substances of choice and numbers of users identified in the 2009 government study are:

- Alcohol   17.1M
- Marijuana   4.3M
- Pain relievers   1.85M
- Cocaine   1.1M
- Tranquilizers   .48M
- Heroin   .399M
- Stimulants   .37M
- Hallucinogens   .37M
- Inhalants   .16M
- Sedatives   .14M

The above figures from the National Survey on Drug Use and Health reflect only a fraction of the data available about alcohol and drug use/abuse. For more information, the reader is directed to http://oas.samhsa.gov/nhsda.htm.

WHY DO ADDICTS STAY HOOKED?

Clearly, the problem is epidemic. So why do so many addicts walk among us? Why don't they get help?

A treatable disease is a far cry from a treated disease. Most addicts don't want help—at least they try to convince themselves they don't. The "gotta have it" drive is so strong that all other thoughts are suppressed. Deep inside, the addict may know he or she needs to stop using, but the innate urge to survive has been defined by pills or alcohol. The brain sends a message that a pill or a drink must be ingested or the addict will perish.

Some days the addict may be able to question rationally, "Why can't I stop?" Looking around, seeing "normal" people, hints of the life that could be, but the craving for relief from emotional or physical pain is unbearable. Feeling better is so simple—a few more pills, one more bottle of wine, or a few shots of whiskey. When the euphoria wears off, the fear, the pain, and the low self-esteem hit so forcefully the addict continues the vicious cycle.

Many times, family, friends, and co-workers are oblivious to the pain and the self-inflicted, bad choices the addict makes to deal with life. Three addicts illustrate this failure to see or address abuse: Frank functioned normally in his role as a high school counselor—no one knew that every night he drank until he was unconscious. No one perceived he couldn't live with the death of his 11-year-old son without the cushion of alcohol. Sally's hip surgery long behind her, she was a functioning attorney despite her inability to forego the pills she once took for pain but now took to survive. For years, Van came to work half loaded, and although some suspected he was drinking on the job, no one dared to confront him.

Addicts are all around us: The young man who packs our groceries at the check-out line; the enormously rich professional football player; the banker who approves our mortgage; the cute college cheerleader; the attractive woman next door; the professor teaching in the local university; the child sitting next to ours in the classroom. Plucking the petals from a daisy, we can recite the old rhyme: Rich man, poor man, beggar man, thief; doctor, lawyer, merchant, chief. There are addicts among all of them.

What do they have in common? Each lives with a disease from which there is no known cure. And typically, they blame their surroundings and others for their problems. They feel powerless over their addiction, and their lives are unmanageable. Under the influence of alcohol or drugs, they live in another world, their consciences dulled and their thoughts twisted. Without treatment, they stay hooked by a compulsive and progressive illness whose terminal point has few options: jails, institutions, or death.

Eventually, the disease takes its toll. Somewhere down the river of addiction, a person begins to drown. If someone does not pull the line in and remove the hook, the person will die.

CHAPTER 2

THE DOWNWARD SPIRAL

Sylvia

amazingly, I managed to complete a degree in respiratory therapy while I was taking more than 25 hydrocodones and 10-15 Zanax a day. It was tough. Depressed and nervous, I wanted to quit, but I kept hearing Don's mocking voice, telling me I would never finish. I was determined to prove him wrong, so I kept pushing my way through the darkness. A walking zombie, somehow I went to class every day, my befuddled mind taking too much time to understand the equations and formulas but finally figuring them out. I would go home after class and collapse on the sofa, unable to keep my eyes open. Around midnight, I would rouse myself and study, then take more pain killers so I could sleep. I still can't believe I finished the degree and passed my board exams. A power higher than I must have processed the information for me. I certainly didn't have enough control of my mind to do it myself.

After graduation, I began working at Hutcheson Medical Center in Ft. Oglethorpe, Ga. Proud to have a good-paying position after so many years of scraping by, I wanted to do a first-rate job. But the 12-hour shifts were tough on my degenerative disk disease, and the back pain from standing and walking on hard floors was almost unbearable. I required more and more medication to function, and even my new wages weren't enough to buy all of the pills I needed. I started stealing money from patients' rooms and taking prescriptions from charts that were written for patients who were being discharged. I then took them to the hospital pharmacist, telling him I was picking up the pills for a patient. I felt guilty, but I was desperate. And then the inevitable happened—I was caught. Disgraced again.

Unbelievably, I was able to get a job at another hospital—and another and another and another. The pattern was always the same—I stole from nurses' lockers, patients' rooms, and sneaked prescriptions from charts. I knew the repercussions, but the pain and the cravings were so intense I shoved them to the back of my mind. My depression worsened as I worked in a place where so many people suffered and died every day, and I plunged into a shadowy, hopeless place. At the last hospital, unable to face being fired again, knowing it was inevitable, I quit my job. For months after that, I just sat at home, staring into space. I was taking so many pills I felt like a sleepwalker, and I found few pleasures in life. All I ever had on my mind were pills and how to get them. Like Joan Collins, who was also afflicted with depression and addiction, there were "many nights I thought I wouldn't make it back out of the dog's dark cave, many days when the sunlight didn't make any difference." Collins described exactly how I felt: "I struggled with the black apparition [of depression]. I could feel it hover, feel its claws tighten on my throat, my heart, defying every rational thought, making a mockery of optimism, of good fortune, of anything true and valuable and real."

I abused drugs, and I abused food—the only pleasure I had in life was eating, and I let food control me, just as I did those little pills. I used drugs to survive and food to placate my grieving spirit. It became my way of life. Slowly, day by day, I cut myself off from the outside world. My days became a blur. I could no longer hide my addiction from my family.

Kacie

I could never put into words how terrible it was to watch my mom destroy her life. Words like "worried" or "frustrated" don't even begin to describe how her abuse affected me. It almost felt like it was sucking the breath out of me. Like my heart truly was breaking into tiny pieces. Like my brain was being suffocated and couldn't think of anything but her and how I could fix her.

I remember watching her iron at night. I would sit on the tub in her bathroom and watch her sway back and forth with her eyes closed. I would stay to make sure she didn't fall over. I usually wondered if she even knew I was in there. I would yell at her to wake up and she would yell back that she was just thinking with her eyes shut. Her eyes gave away her secret. She's always been the most bright-eyed person I know. Those droopy, glazed-over eyes could never fool me.

I started checking on her every night while she was sleeping, multiple times, just to make sure she was still breathing. Everywhere she went, I called to make sure she arrived and hadn't dozed off while driving. I started *telling her to say her prayers at night, hoping God would remember to not let her overdose.*

I knew I couldn't make her change or make her stop taking pills, but at least I could try to keep her safe.

Stacie

I had a million different emotions as I watched mom on drugs. Sometimes I was mad. Other times I was sad. Some days I felt like I hated her (although I really didn't), and others I would feel so sorry for her I would break down. I knew she was better than the person who was taking drugs and stealing. That wasn't the mom I remembered—the classiest, smartest, most beautiful woman around. I was always so proud of her. But she changed. She gained a lot of weight. And, it was embarrassing to go places with her because she was so groggy—like she was half asleep. I constantly worried something was going to happen to her when she was driving—I was scared to death she would wreck and kill herself or someone else. I also worried she would overdose, either accidentally or intentionally. When I woke up every morning, I prayed the whole way down the stairs she wouldn't be lying in her bed dead because she had taken too many pills. Then I would stand in her bedroom door and check to see if she was breathing. Thank goodness she always was.

Sherry

We all knew Sylvia was taking way too many drugs, but we had no idea how many. What we did know for sure was that Sylvia had to get help or she was going to die. Her two daughters, her son, and my sister Flavia and I talked about what we should do and together decided an inpatient treatment facility was our best hope. With no insurance for Sylvia, our choices were limited, and we settled on New Life Lodge in Burns, Tn. When we all confronted Sylvia and told her we had made arrangements for her admission, she adamantly denied she was addicted and insisted she could stop taking the drugs. We were just as insistent that she needed help, and although she resisted with all her strength, we forced her to go to New Life Lodge.

Bart

Although I watched my mother turn into a person I didn't know, I still didn't realize she was addicted until she went to New Life Lodge. I kept thinking she would get better—and she would tell us she was better, but then she would get worse again. Even when she acted normally for a few days, I knew it would be just a matter of time until she was droopy-eyed again. I was relieved when she went for treatment, thinking she would finally get better for good.

Sylvia

Those were the worst eight weeks of my life. I was coming off both hyrodocodone and Zanax, and it was so bad for the first seven weeks I thought I was dying. The one medicine I was given for withdrawals caused a rash all over my body, so it was discontinued. By the second day I felt so weak I couldn't walk. Then my voice became so faint I could only talk in a whisper. I didn't sleep at all for 14 days while I was detoxing—I couldn't lay still long enough to fall asleep. I felt ants crawling all over me. Heat radiated through my body and then out my skin until I thought I was on fire. My detox room was only a few feet from the nurses' station, and I drove them crazy all night, begging for help. One night I was so distraught a nurse called Sherry, and she came to the treatment center and stayed with me for several hours. I pleaded with her, trying to persuade her to take me home, but she refused. I was so angry she wouldn't do what I wanted I started hitting her hands with my fists. I didn't want to hurt her, but I was desperate to convince her I needed to get out of that place. Finally, the nurses told her it would be better if she left, and I was again alone with my demons.

After 14 days, I started falling asleep from exhaustion, but my body would jerk, waking me up. The flames felt like they were still coming from my body, and the few minutes I did sleep I had hallucinations of burning alive in a fire. My blood pressure climbed dangerously high, and my heart beat so fast and hard I thought it might burst. All I wanted to do was go home so I could feel better. But no one would help me. Defeated, I threw my clothes in my bag and dragged it along with me down to the cabin so I could start the classes they said I had to take before I could leave. Even though I was trying to do what they wanted me to do, it was hard because I wasn't sleeping but a couple of hours each night.

One day, desperate to escape, I called a cab; but when the taxi driver arrived, I didn't have any money for the three-hour journey home. I begged him to take me to Chattanooga and I would give him money when we arrived, even though I had none and had no way to get any. He looked at me like I was an idiot and left, so I started walking down the road and when I couldn't walk, I crawled. When I couldn't go any further, I staggered up to a house and collapsed in the yard. The man who lived there called the lodge, and they sent someone to pick me up.

Looking back, I can't believe I acted so crazily—but that was just the beginning. I was frantic. The whole time I was at New Life Lodge, I had never felt so weird and wretched in all my life. I learned about addiction during those weeks, but mainly I learned I never wanted to take Zanax again. By the time I left, I wasn't feeling much better (I had withdrawal symptoms, mainly from the Zanax, for four or five months and still didn't feel normal), but I thought I had my drug problem licked.

Sherry

We had all tried to support Sylvia, and she would periodically seem better for a while before she slipped back into higher and higher doses of medication. It was awful to watch her slowly kill herself. From a beautiful, active person she was disintegrating into the depths of a life we had never seen. We saw the ravages of her drug problem on her face, but we couldn't see into her heart and mind—we couldn't understand how the pain could be so bad she would let herself fall apart. It was a long time before we realized she couldn't just "fix" herself. When that insight finally took hold, we knew we had to get her help—nothing we had been doing was making her any better.

Trying to get Sylvia to agree to go into treatment was tumultuous. She didn't think she needed treatment; we did. She thought she could stop taking drugs by herself; we knew she wanted to but couldn't. It took tears and threats from all of us to force her to go. I realize now that because Sylvia did not willingly go into treatment, it was hard for her to benefit from it.

Watching her and talking to her by phone during the weeks of withdrawal (and even the months after she returned home) was painful, but it told us what a strong hold the drugs had on her and how hard it was to fight against the hook that was piercing the very lifeblood out of her. The night the nurses called me to the treatment center, my heart broke as I watched Sylvia's body convulsing in agony. When she begged me to take her home, and I knew I couldn't, I cried as she cried, hurting for her and with her. And I understood how desperate she was when she took my two hands and pounded her fists into them as she pleaded with me to take her home. Weeks later, when she had finished the treatment, I was relieved that she was on the road to recovery. She had written each of us—her three children, Flavia, and me—letters asking us to forgive her and continue to support her. We responded with love, and hope sprang into our hearts that Sylvia's nightmare with drugs was behind her. We prayed she would apply what she had learned at the treatment center when she returned home. But it wasn't over.

WHAT ARE THE SIGNS A PERSON HAS BEEN HOOKED?

Family and co-workers sometimes recognize the signs of addiction before the addict does. If a person complains of vague symptoms to get more medication, sees several doctors and/or pharmacies to get more pills, or uses prescription pills prescribed for others, chances are the person is hooked. Emotional signals, such as isolation, crying spells, depression, resentment, hostility, dishonesty, and mood swings may be of concern to family and friends but seem normal to a person who sees such negative emotions as common reactions to a disappointing life. And seldom does the addict tie his or her physical problems to the addiction.

Even if the addict admits a problem, justification undergirds the denial. The addict may say, "I only take the pills when I am upset." "When the boss attacks me, I have to take something to calm down." "I am so sad and lonely, I would die if I didn't take the pills." "When I feel a panic attack coming on, I have to take a couple of pills." "You can't imagine how terrible my pain is." Excuses and explanations like these come freely from the mouths of addicts. They convince themselves but rarely do they convince others close to them—at least not for long.

Addicts may also show resentment that anyone would question them. "It's none of your business how many pills I take." "Get off my back. I can take care of myself." "Why don't you leave me alone? I feel bad enough without your condemning me." And, addicts often take pills to submerge the guilt they feel for what they do when they have had too many. That, too, justifies the abuse: "I need the pills to make me feel better about myself."

Excessive drugs make a person feel invincible. When I had enough Zanax and hydrocodone, I thought I could walk into a patient's room and not get caught, Sylvia says. *I began to shoplift at Walmart and other places to avoid spending my 'pill money' on groceries or other necessities. When I wasn't caught, my feeling of invincibility increased—that is, until I was caught and went through the humiliation of being handcuffed and arrested.*

When family or friends confront the addict after such incidents, the addict frequently becomes defensive, turning the anger they feel toward themselves at the very people who are trying to help. Sylvia was sometimes overcome with guilt when she woke up and saw things she had stolen but couldn't remember taking. But the cravings were stronger than her remorse, and more pills brought more bravery and more insolence. When family members questioned where she got the money for a closet filled with expensive clothes, accessories for her house, or gifts for her children, she would strike back in anger, accusing them of not trusting her. Turning the guilt back on the accuser helped ward off suspicions and helped soften Sylvia's self-reproach.

HOW DO YOU HELP SOMEONE WHO IS HOOKED?

Unfortunately, until addicts are ready to face their problems, helping them is almost impossible. When forced into treatment, the resentment and anger continue, diminishing the positive benefits. As long as the addict is in denial, saying, "I don't have a problem," recovery can't begin.

Eventually, when the addict goes from functional denial, when he or she can still function normally despite too many pills or alcohol, to dysfunctional denial, family and friends see the denial for what it is. When an addict denies a problem despite difficulty waking up or barely remembering what he or she does each day, control of life has been lost. This can result in marriage problems or divorce, loss of a job, or even criminal acts.

Intervention

The family has no choice—intervene or let the addict continue on her path until she dies. Intervention can be simple and informal, as when Sylvia was confronted by her family. Colvin describes a number of other options, including a different type of intervention when a professional interventionist works with an addict. He describes how one such interventionist works, explaining that Bruce Cotter recognizes the worst thing you can do is try to tell an addict what to do. "'They won't buy it. I want them to make the decision to seek treatment and then I support their decision.'" Cotter believes private interventions—between a trained professional and an addict—work better than having a group confront an individual. "'People I work with are scared, angry, confused, and paranoid. They're despairing, they're hurting, and they feel guilty. So I find I can work more effectively with them alone....'"

Colvin also describes a group approach, a structured intervention in which a team of people (three to eight family members and friends, and sometimes a counselor) organize and plan not only a meeting with the addict but also make all arrangements for the admission of the addict to a treatment center as soon as the meeting is concluded. This group also pre-plans responses to the addict's reasons for not being able to go immediately into treatment. If a pet must be cared for, arrangements have been made in advance. If a leave of absence from a job is required, someone on the intervention team has handled that. Whatever argument the addict makes, the team has an answer and a plan. In addition, each of the members of the intervention team reads a personal letter to the addict, telling him or her how the addiction is affecting not only the addict but also friends, family, and co-workers. The letters include "facts," evidence that the person's addiction is affecting their wellness and their relationships. Then, hopefully with the concurrence of the addict, someone drives the person to the treatment center.

Whichever form of intervention is used, addicts need help. Self-diagnosis would be preferable, but most are incapable of facing reality. Hooked, they are powerless and paralyzed in their addiction. Without outside pressure, most addicts will continue on their road of destruction. With help, the road to recovery can begin. But it's an uphill climb.

Treatment Centers

How does an addict or his family find a place that matches the individual's needs and ability to pay? Local hospitals, primary care physicians, psychiatrists, and religious leaders can usually make recommendations. Another excellent resource can be found at this Web site: http://findtreatment.samhsa.gov/. It is a searchable directory of more than 11,000 programs around the country that treat substance abuse addictions. The facility locator found on this Web site includes outpatient treatment programs, residential treatment programs, hospital inpatient programs, and partial hospitalization/day treatment programs.

Although some addicts are tempted to detox at home, the advantages of a treatment facility to begin recovery are critical. Not only do they provide medical supervision of withdrawal symptoms and vital signs, but they also offer medication management, support groups, suicide watches, and a non-judgmental environment. Moreover, they deliver the basic lessons needed for long-term recovery after detoxification.

But to get to that point, detox must be survived, and it can be terrifying, especially for those who have been addicted for long periods of time and those who take medicines for both pain and psychiatric problems. The longer the abuse and the larger the amount consumed, the more extended and more severe the withdrawal symptoms. The acute level of detoxification typically lasts four to seven days, but the symptoms (at a lesser level of intensity) can continue for weeks or even months. These symptoms include chills, sweats, nausea, vomiting, shakiness, anxiety, fatigue, restlessness, headache, muscle pain, seizures, depression, and rage.

Although some, like Sylvia, will never forget the horrors of withdrawal, others may want to keep a journal describing the terror and agony. Reading the journal when tempted to abuse again is a powerful deterrent.

After detox, it's not unusual for an addict to mistrust the medical and counseling workers at a treatment facility. First, these people let the addict go through purgatory, and even if they tried to appear sympathetic, they must not have really cared or they would have done something to stop the torture—or so the addict reasons. Second, it's hard for addicts to open up, to share their deepest fears and thoughts with counselors or with other addicts. Many times the addict feels, "I'm not like the other people here. I'm a better person. I just got on the wrong track and couldn't get off, but that doesn't make me crazy like these other patients. Besides, some of the patients just use drugs to get high, to feel good. I used them because I was in terrible pain, physically or emotionally." Many times, the addict differentiates himself from others he sees as common junkies, pill-heads, dope fiends, etc.

In short, the addict thinks, "I am unique. No one can help me, because my life and my problems are different from others."

Just as an addict tries to convince himself he is dissimilar to other addicts, he finds it difficult to admit he stole or manipulated others to get drugs. In an unaltered state of mind, he would never have done such things, so he rationalizes that makes them less wrong. Defending himself keeps feelings of embarrassment and guilt at bay. While truth and reality need to penetrate the barriers of self-defense, admitting who he has become isn't easy. If the addict can get beyond denial, recovery can begin.

Narcotics/Alcoholics Anonymous

Many programs follow the treatment template of the Narcotics Anonymous (NA) and Alcoholics Anonymous (AA) twelve-step model, which has helped more than one million people since its inception. In a group with other addicts, a person no longer has to feel alone. No matter what the past thoughts or actions, others have felt and done the same. Within the safe environment at NA or AA, an addict is confronted with these three realities:

- I am powerless over addiction, and my life is unmanageable.
- Although I am not responsible for my own disease, I am responsible for my recovery.
- I can no longer blame people, places, and situations for my addiction. I must face my own problems and feelings.

NA also helps addicts recognize they are "critically ill, not hopelessly bad." Moreover, the disease "can only be arrested through abstinence." To achieve abstinence, addicts must change themselves—not the people or circumstances around them. In that framework, NA teaches, addicts re-find their self-respect and sense of self-worth.

Although the twelve steps are readily available, because of the magnitude of their insight and impact on long-term recovery, they are provided below:

1. We admitted that we were powerless over our addiction, that our lives had become unmanageable.
2. We came to believe that a Power greater than ourselves could restore us to sanity.
3. We made a decision to turn our will and our lives over to the care of God as we understood Him.
4. We made a searching and fearless moral inventory of ourselves.
5. We admitted to God, to ourselves, and to another human being the exact nature of our wrongs.
6. We were entirely ready to have God remove all these defects of character.
7. We humbly asked Him to remove our shortcomings.
8. We made a list of all persons we had harmed and became willing to make amends to them all.
9. We made direct amends to such people wherever possible except when to do so would injure them or others.
10. We continued to take personal inventory and when we were wrong promptly admitted it.
11. We sought through prayer and meditation to improve our conscious contact with God as we understood Him, praying only for knowledge of His will for us and the power to carry that out.
12. Having had a spiritual awakening as a result of these steps, we tried to carry this message to addicts, and to practice these principles in all our affairs.

Admitting they are powerless over drugs or alcohol opens addicts up to accept that their dependence is a physical, mental, and spiritual disease that affects all parts of their lives. NA describes the controlling power this way: "The physical aspect of our disease is the compulsive use of drugs, the inability to stop using once we have started. The mental aspect of our disease is the obsession, or overpowering desire to use, even when we are destroying our lives. The spiritual part of our disease is our total self-centeredness. Denial, substitution, rationalization, justification, distrust of others, guilt, embarrassment, dereliction, degradation, isolation, and loss of control are all results of our disease." And, NA adds, addiction is just that—a disease, not a moral deficiency.

CHAPTER 3

THE VICIOUS CYCLE

Sylvia

After I finished treatment at New Life Lodge, I found employment in a dental office. It was devastating not to be able to use my new degree, and, even worse, the dental office paid less than half what I earned in respiratory therapy. Added to this disappointment was continuing withdrawal from Xanax. Even after 10 weeks, I still experienced symptoms and felt exhausted. Despite the shakes, nervousness, and weakness, I managed to stay off drugs for about six months. Even when the dentist I worked for gave me a prescription for hydrocodones because I had a bad toothache, I tore it up, determined not to start down into the black hole again. But a few days later, after a root canal, he gave me another prescription, and this time I had it filled.

Addiction had been held in abeyance as long as I didn't take the first pill, but it was still there, like a time bomb. All it took was one spark, and it exploded. I was hooked again. Soon, I was stealing whole prescription pads from the dentist. I'd fill them in, forge the dentist's name and take them to different pharmacies to have them filled. Sometimes I called in prescriptions from the dental office as if I were doing it for a patient. My brain circuits were too cross-wired by this time to think rationally, so I believed the pharmacies wouldn't realize what I was doing. Once again, I thought I was invincible. Soon, arrested and charged with ten felonies, I crash landed. I was thankful there weren't more charges—there could have been.

Coming home after New Life Lodge had been hard. All of my problems were still there to be faced, and all it took was one pill to make them go away. Or, so I told myself. The root canal just gave me the justification I needed to use drugs to take away the mental pain. I couldn't get the yearning for release out of my head. No one understood how I felt. At least at New Life Lodge others knew what cravings do to you. People who haven't been hooked have no idea how it feels to have your brain convince you a pill will help you get through your problems. And, because I had been in treatment out of town, I didn't have a local support system already in place. Of course, I thought I didn't need one (I could stay off drugs by myself, I believed), so I didn't try to get involved in a Narcotics Anonymous group. So here I was again. Caught. In jail. Embarrassed and humiliated. Ashamed to face my kids.

Bart

When I found out mom was stealing, I thought, "She really went over the edge this time." It finally sank in my head that she was so hooked on drugs she would do almost anything to get money. Still, I didn't understand why she couldn't just give up the drugs and go back to being normal. I knew she was addicted, but in my mind it was like being addicted to cigarettes. I had no idea how hard it would be for her to stay off drugs.

WHAT COMPELS THE ADDICT TO GET HOOKED AGAIN?

Relapse. An addict hopes and prays it won't happen, but if the source of the person's problems isn't addressed, slipping back into abuse is almost inevitable. In the safe environment of a treatment center, commitments to remain free of drugs or alcohol flow freely. But in the real world, where family conflicts continue, physical problems persist, and daily life holds no happiness or a better life for tomorrow, the pills hold a seductive charm. Dangling from the hook, they promise escape from the perilous waters of life. The addict thinks, "I'll just take one [drink or pill] to make me feel better, and then I won't take any more." But addiction is a zero tolerance disease. The "gottta have it" craving is never suppressed with just one. NA teaches that one is too many and a thousand never enough. Refusing to take the first drink or the first pill is the only way to keep from returning to active addiction.

Some addiction specialists believe relapse after treatment is more likely if the person resisted help and was forced to enter a facility. From the get-go, motivation is diminished as the addict persists, at least in his own mind, with declaring no help is needed. Even if the addict has entered treatment without screaming and kicking but grudgingly, the commitment to get help is often because others want the person to do it, not because he wants to do it for himself. For example, an addict may enter treatment to keep his spouse from leaving. The threat of losing a child is another strong incentive. Or, the impetus may be trying to avoid going to jail. In some cases, after a hearing or trial, the court ordered the person to go through treatment.

If the addict did not accept the need for treatment and did not participate fully (especially emotionally) in the process, the motivation to continue in after-programs or support groups is diminished. This can result from the feeling that "I'm not like those other people," reflecting a sense of superiority, or more likely, an unwillingness to accept that he is like other addicts in the most important way: inability to live without substance abuse. Or, it can come from overconfidence: "I've learned what causes me to take drugs, and I've recovered." What the addict doesn't realize is that "recovered" isn't the same as "cured." He learned about drug addiction but not about relapse. Until the addict wants to be drug free more than he wants the drugs—until he realizes that the drugs keep him living in misery—he isn't going to stay in recovery.

Triggers

Learning about relapse requires an awareness of the triggers that push an addict to bite the hook again. While each person has a specific set of triggers, they can typically be characterized as people, places, objects, and the addict's own mood. Within those categories, individuals must identify their unique issues that give them an excuse to relapse. These are sometimes called "relapse justifications"—the addict's brain finds ways to give him permission to move toward drugs or alcohol. After a trigger, let's say a father's disagreement with his teenage daughter, he feels stressed. Thoughts become arguments; rational thoughts fight with addictive thoughts. Inside the addict's head, the debate drags on between his desire to stay clean and his need to escape the tension. The latter part of this debate stimulates cravings, and memories of past relief surge in the brain. If the craving becomes overpowering, the addict reaches for a pill or a drink, and relapse occurs.

Factors Affecting Relapse

Gorski (2008) studied the three facets of addiction that affect not only initiation but also relapse: biological, psychological and social dependence. Addicts can be dependent on one or more of these levels at the same time—the more levels involved, the more likely the addict will relapse.

Biological dependence relates to physical dependence. The physical attribute causes issues with tolerance and withdrawals: The more an addict ingests, the more she needs to reach previous levels of physical relief. Her system raises the tolerance level as she increases the dosage or consumption. When the abuse stops, the body rebels and withdrawal symptoms crop up in protest for what the body craves but is not getting.

Psychological dependence occurs when a person relies on drugs or alcohol to help control her thinking, feeling, and behavior. Without the substance of choice, the person believes she cannot think rationally or clearly. (Ironically, the drugs or alcohol cause irrational thinking.) The addict cannot deal with her feelings without the chemical infusion that numbs the brain or makes her brave enough to deal with life or to do whatever it takes to get the substance needed. In an altered state of mind, the addict justifies her actions or behavior, often blaming others for her problems.

Social dependence refers to the need for alcohol or drugs to interact, live, and work with others. Gorski calls it a necessity for lubricating or facilitating social behavior, adding that without the abuse, the addict cannot maintain satisfactory relationships with others.

Stages of Relapse

Even though the names are different and they are ordered differently, the three stages of relapse mirror the three kinds of dependence. Melemis (2010), in his book, *I Want to Change My Life*, emphasizes that relapse is a process, not an event. It starts long before the addict falls into the chasm of relapse, sometimes weeks or months in advance.

The process begins with emotional relapse. In this stage, the person is not focused on using, but his emotions and behaviors set him up for a possible relapse in the future. Melemis identifies a number of signs of emotional relapse, including anxiety, intolerance, anger, defensiveness, mood swings, isolation, not asking for help, and not going to meetings.

When several of these signs are present, the addict must recognize he is in emotional relapse and change his behavior. The first step is to realize he may be isolating himself and ask for help. If anxiety is a problem, relaxation techniques may help. Poor sleeping and eating habits must also be addressed. Melemis cautions if behavior isn't attended to at this stage, the addict becomes exhausted and his emotions compel him to try to escape. This moves the addict into mental relapse.

The battle to use or not to use begins in the mental relapse stage. Part of the addict wants to use, but part of her doesn't. Over a period of time, the addict moves from an idle thought, musing about using, to a more concrete thought that is a definite movement toward using. One sign of mental relapse is thinking about people and places where using occurred in the past. Glamorizing past use is another signal, as are lying and making plans for how to obtain the drug of choice.

To combat mental relapse, Melemis suggests the addict play a tape in her mind of the full cycle of slipping back into addiction. When her mind says she can get away with using, that no one will find out, she must remind herself of previous negative consequences and potential ramifications that will be the likely outcome of relapse. The addict must remember if she could control her craving after just one drink or one pill, she would have done it before. Melemis also urges the addict to tell someone she has the urge to use—a friend, a supporter, a family member, or someone in recovery. Sharing helps get the urge out of the person's system.

In addition, the addict can distract himself by doing something—going for a walk, shopping, or visiting a friend. When relapse threatens, he shouldn't just sit there. Urges usually last only 15 to 30 minutes, even though it feels like an eternity, so if the addict can postpone responding to the craving by being physically active, it will help.

If the addict succumbs to emotional and mental relapse, Melemis avers, physical relapse isn't far away. It's not rocket science. If the addict can't resist the craving, he will get in his car and drive to the liquor store or to his dealer. Relapse is almost impossible to stop at that point. Few addicts, once they have started toward the physical substance, will be able to force themselves to stop and turn around. The key to recovery is for the addict to catch himself before he gets to this point. That's often easier than it sounds. Dealing with complicated emotional issues that may have haunted the addict for years takes skills the person may not have. The only way he knows to survive is to get the physical relief that addiction brings. Grabbing the bait dangling from the hook is easier and faster than getting to the root of the problem (familial, financial, or otherwise).

Sylvia

So here I sit again. Waiting for someone to bail me out. Facing my family, knowing how disgusted and embarrassed they are, weighs on my heart like an anchor, pulling me back into the black sea of depression.

This time it was even harder to convince my family to help me. They wanted to leave me in jail, hoping that might wake me up.

I made it through court and managed to get off with probation, probably with God's grace, although I don't know why He would want to help me since I had turned my back on Him so many times. Thankful, I promised Him, my kids, and myself I would never take another pill.

Unable to find a job, I went to work for my former in-laws, who were elderly and not in good health. I loved them and worked hard trying to make their lives more comfortable and enjoyable. I cooked and cleaned every day, bought their groceries, made special desserts, and ensured they took their medications. I had no intention of ever hurting them, but as usual when you're a drug addict, you end up doing things you don't want to do. Being in the home where I had had many happy times with my kids and ex-husband wasn't easy for me. I started grieving more and more for my family and yearned for us to be together again. It broke my heart that no one came to see my ex in-laws anymore, and I knew if my family were still together it all would be different, just like everything else in my life.

I fought the depression for a while, but when Christmas came and I drove home at night alone, knowing my ex-husband lived a few miles away with his new family, I didn't care anymore. I needed something to help me get through the holiday songs and lights and going home alone to an empty house. I just planned to take hydrocodones through Christmas and then I'd stop.

The only problem was it was beginning to take increasing numbers to have the same effect that it did before. I started out taking one-half to one pill, then two or three, then four, and on and on. I was going to four or five doctors at the same time, but I needed so many pills I was running out of doctors to prescribe them. Then I discovered I could order them off the Internet. It was easy. A doctor (at least he said he was a doctor) would call, ask a few questions, and then a package of 90 or 120 hydrocodones was delivered in two to three days. To meet my growing need, I began ordering from five different websites at one time. Then they either caught on or started going out of business, and I would have to find new sources.

AUTHORS' NOTE: *Despite the Drug Enforcement Administration (DEA) regulations implementing the Ryan Haight Online Pharmacy Consumer Protection Act of 2008, one pharmacy, combined with another online group, shipped 30,000 packages of prescription drugs across the country during the first six months of 2010—no prescriptions required. The two pharmacies were part of a large ring of at least 200 websites that act as internet pharmacies, selling prescription drugs without valid prescriptions. A year later, in 2011, a quick click, click, click on the Internet turned up 14 sites selling hydrocodones without prescriptions. A few more clicks found ample sources for other pain killers, anti-anxiety drugs, and other addictive drugs.*

Sylvia

In my mind, I didn't see all drug addicts as being the same, and I never thought of myself as having the typical life of addiction. I had never taken the hard drugs, used needles, or snorted. I just took my pills with water (the simplest way), so I thought I could stop whenever I wanted. If I had been around people who took harder or stronger drugs, I'm sure I would have taken them too. But I was a drug addict who used alone, who lived in my own little world, who didn't spend time with other addicts. Still, I have learned that a drug addict is a drug addict no matter how or where she chooses to take prescription or illegal drugs—whether they are snorted, injected with needles, or chewed up and swallowed. It doesn't matter whether a person takes them to get high, to party with friends, or to escape problems or pain. They always spark the same kind of problems, however you choose to ingest them or whatever the environment.

During this time I was arrested several times for shoplifting—not for things I needed but because my brain was so numb by this time I didn't care. The worse I felt about myself, the more I wanted to steal. Makes no sense, but nothing I did made any sense.

Then, when I was at the depth of my depression, I discovered a Certificate of Deposit with several hundred thousand dollars in it at my in-laws' house. I didn't think about stealing that day, but later, when I became desperate, needing pills and money for my kids, I went to the bank and lied, telling them my mother-in-law sent me to withdraw five thousand dollars. The manager who approved the transaction didn't even question me because I had gone to high school with her, and the Sylvia she knew would never take someone else's money. Since it was so easy, when that was gone (and it didn't last long because I was paying so much for pills), I went back for five thousand more and then ten thousand, then more and more over a period of three to four months. The worse I felt about myself, the more pills I needed and the more money I needed to buy them. I was so ashamed for deceiving a friend and stealing from my family, but I felt so hopeless and helpless I didn't know how else to survive.

I don't know whether I'm just unlucky or stupid (probably both), but I got caught again and was charged with my 11th felony, this time for stealing $45,000. In a mind controlled by drugs, I justified this by telling myself I deserved the money since my ex-husband had built a new house, a large horse barn, and later a swimming pool, as well as taking trips, yet he wasn't paying me the alimony he owed me. I always found a way to defend what I did.

Thankfully, I was able to work out a plea bargain by paying back the money. I sold my house to get part of it, and my sister Sherry paid the remainder with the condition that I go back into treatment.

Stacie

It was hard knowing my mom stole anything and everything—clothes, food, money, and whatever else she thought we needed or wanted. Every Christmas when I saw the room full of gifts, I realized they were probably stolen. I was just thankful she managed to avoid jail. Then, when she took the money from my dad's parents, I knew this time imprisonment was likely inevitable. If that happened, I was scared to death she wouldn't come back out—that she would kill herself in jail.

Kacie

I knew my mom was stealing "things" throughout the years she was on drugs. Items maybe we couldn't afford or maybe didn't even realize she was stealing because she had taken too many pills that day. I didn't know she was stealing to buy drugs until I was 24. Our world came crashing down in May 2005. She had been taking care of my dad's parents because their health was declining. My dad's sister found out my mom had taken over $40,000 of my grandparents' money over the course of a few months to buy pills, and I knew my dad's siblings were not going to have mercy on my mother. I was devastated. I thought that was it for my mom. I thought I would be visiting her in jail for the next 20 years. I was heartbroken and scared.

The day she turned herself in was the hardest day of my life. I thought it was going to be fairly painless...she would turn herself it, post bail, and be out within a few hours. My aunts had a different plan. I got off work that afternoon thinking I would call her cell phone and she would answer. But there was no answer. I called my sister who told me no one was bailing her out that day. They were going to try "tough love," something I don't believe in. I believe in love, and it should never be tough. I was able to visit her the next day and she was hysterical. Talking to my mom through that glass window while holding that awful jail telephone and watching her scream, cry, and beg was hands down the most painful thing I've ever experienced. I went outside and had the biggest meltdown of my life. I knew I had to find a way to bail her out, and I didn't care who got mad at me for it. My mom would never leave me whether she was on pills or not, and I wasn't about to leave her in that place. I bailed her out later that day with the help of some friends and family. She went to rehab the next day.

Sylvia

My family wanted me to return to New Life Lodge, but I wanted to go to a treatment center in my home town. Both my sisters were upset with me because I had been bailed out of jail, and because I didn't go to the treatment center they had chosen. I had no communication with either of them the three weeks I was in rehab and very little after I got out. I felt like I was being punished and didn't feel any support from them. Maybe they were trying their "tough love," but it made me feel all alone and scared to death. I guess they were just sick of me and didn't know what to do anymore. Since I didn't have their support, I had to beg the treatment center to admit me because I had no money. I tried hard to benefit from the counseling this time, and when I finished the inpatient program, I was determined to stay clean.

I started applying for jobs, but when I told them of my arrests, they said they would be in touch; and, of course, I never heard from them. Then, in desperation, I lied to a temporary service about my record and was hired for a doctor's office. Three weeks later, the same day my office manager told me I was doing a good job and was being hired permanently, the temporary agency called and told her of my omission on the application, so she fired me instead. I broke down sobbing and cried all the way to my car and all the way home, knowing I had lost another job and had to tell my family. At least I wasn't fired for stealing or taking drugs. But no one would believe me.

After that, I hid at home, hibernating. I had gotten to the point I had to take pills to get up in the morning. I didn't want to go anywhere or do anything. Even worse, I couldn't even handle talking with my kids on the phone without a pill. Beaten down by a hideous monster, I wanted to curl up and die.

After sitting in my apartment for months, totally dependent on my family for support, my niece got me a job as a custodian at the accounting firm where she worked. Although utterly humiliated, I was grateful to have a job and worked really hard—and I cut way back on the pills so I could function. During that time my sister Sherry moved back to town, and I moved in with her and her husband because I wasn't making enough money to live independently. This just made me feel more worthless about myself.

I felt like a loser. Here I was, 54 years old, cleaning toilets and mopping floors and living with my sister. And to think I used to spend my days playing tennis, eating lunch with my friends, and shopping. My self-esteem hit rock bottom, and combined with back pain from cleaning a 25,000 square foot building every night, I convinced myself I had a reason to take more and more pain killers to survive. I was smart enough not to get back on Zanax— not only had I learned they made my depression worse instead of better, I knew I NEVER wanted to go through withdrawals from them again. But I was dumb enough to think the pain killers helped me and that I had to have them.

As usual, I told myself I would just take enough pills to make it for now, and I could quit when my life got better. And then I was given a wonderful opportunity, and I thought it had actually gotten better. I was offered the position of Administrative Assistant to the managing partner of the accounting firm. I don't know if someone felt sorry for me or if God intervened on my behalf, but I was determined to prove I could do the job. At first, my boss seemed like a kind man—he told me I was now part of the company family and even gave me money to buy clothes for office work since I hadn't worked in that environment in recent years. In turn, I worked harder than I had ever worked in my life. I taught myself the job and was feeling proud of myself that I was doing something right for a change.

My good feelings didn't last long. Soon, I began to feel my boss was never satisfied. It was like he still thought of me as the cleaning lady who wasn't capable of doing anything else, even though I had a degree. Every time he criticized or belittled me, I felt like an idiot. He had no idea that I already felt so bad about myself that even the smallest criticism caused me to fight back tears. No matter how hard I tried, he always made me feel I didn't try hard enough. Sometimes I even got blamed for other people's mistakes. When I tried to explain, he cut me off and dismissed me as if I weren't important enough to be heard, sometimes scolding me like a child when I made a mistake. I had been so excited—so thankful that my boss gave me an opportunity to prove I could do more than clean—but now I thought he was purposefully tearing me down so I would quit. I thought he knew of my drug abuse before I was hired, but maybe he didn't know everything.

As my boss continued to bombard me, putting me under more and more pressure, I had to increase the number of pills to face going to work every day. One morning out of nowhere he told me that he had decided to hire someone to replace me. My heart sank as I thought about having to tell my daughters and family I had screwed up and was jobless again. As much as I tried not to, I broke down sobbing and couldn't stop. And then for some reason, probably pity, he told me I could continue working for him until I found another job. Because of my arrest record, no one else would hire me; but I couldn't face not having a job, so even though my spirit was crushed, I kept going to work each day despite knowing he didn't want me there. It was awful. I felt everyone was laughing at me, wondering why I was still coming to work after being fired. I needed more and more pills to tackle each day.

My self-confidence plummeted to zero, and within days it took 40 pain killers a day for me to be able to force myself to go to work and make it through the day. I was filled with resentment toward my boss and toward life in general. I cried a lot at work, and at home I just sat in my room, filled with fear and disgust that I was hooked again. Only more pills could hold down my guilt that I had started stealing again to pay for the hundreds of pills I needed each week.

I had worked my way through every doctor in town who handed out pills freely, and I was down to only one who would prescribe pain pills for me. It wasn't long before he dismissed me from his practice because the Drug Enforcement Agency was on to him. It was probably good I could no longer go there since the office was so full of drug addicts they had to keep a security guard in the waiting room. Now I had to get all of my pills from a dealer, costing me more money. I was paying six to ten dollars for each of the 40 pills I was taking every day. I was finally coming to the end of my addiction cycle, but I didn't know it.

Bart

I didn't understand my mom's addiction, and I didn't know how to deal with it. I felt sorry for her—that she couldn't control what she was doing—but I was also mad she was doing this to herself and to us. I tried to block it out of my mind, and sometimes I could. But I still worried about her. And I kept thinking, "She will eventually get over this if she doesn't kill herself before that happens." I guess that's why I never talked to my mom about her addiction, but I'm not sure. And I doubt if it would have done any good if I had. I didn't know what to say, so I just didn't talk about it.

Kacie

I continued to watch my mom give more and more of herself to addiction until I was 28. I watched her lose jobs, lose homes, get arrested, risk relationships with loved ones...it was like watching someone suffering a terminal illness, like I was waiting for her to die.

Stacie

My relationship with mom while she was on drugs for 15+ years was a roller coaster ride. Every time I thought she was better, that she was going to stay off drugs, she would relapse and I went careening down a hill. I felt like the only way I could make it through the constant turmoil was to put up a wall and harden myself. At times, I was mad at her because I was trying to make a life of my own and I needed her to be there for me and give me advice—and she wasn't. Not only was I worried that my mom wasn't going to be there to see me get married or have kids, but then when I did have children I was scared to death to trust her with them because she was still abusing drugs. She went into rehab before I had my first child. I was five months pregnant when I found out she had relapsed. I felt betrayed. How could I trust her with my child when her judgment was constantly impaired? I wanted to trust her when she said she was "never going to take pills again," but then she would get caught stealing or forging prescriptions. Every time she stopped abusing drugs, I would slowly start to regain my trust and then something else would happen. Trust shattered over and over made it hard to believe she would ever stay drug-free.

Irrational Thinking

At some point, the addict may not try to hide his unusual behaviors any more since he doesn't even recognize they are abnormal. The thinking of a person who has a high moral code may be so altered that he reasons irrationally: "It's not fair that I don't have everything when everyone else does." Such reasoning justifies stealing. And the pills assuage the fear and the guilt.

Charlie, Jane, and Jennifer exemplified this kind of rationalization. Charlie was so high on OxyContin and cocaine that it didn't bother him to pick up lumber for his boss, stop by his own house and take some off the truck (to sell later). Since his boss had several houses under construction at one time, he never realized Charlie was stealing. Charlie needed the extra money he got from selling the lumber to support his habit and reasoned his boss was rich and could stand the loss.

Jane, a teenager who became hooked after taking uppers at a party, stole from her parents' wallets when she became desperate for money to buy pills. They didn't even notice the money was missing, so they must not need it, she thought. Ironically, they noticed when their own pills were missing, but a hundred dollars or so a week didn't catch their attention.

Jennifer, a nurse, substituted ibuprofen for her hospital patients' narcotics, taking them to feed her drug habit that had begun after back surgery. In her mind, she was doing them a favor—she was keeping them from becoming addicted.

Denials and rationalizations like those used by Charlie, Jane, and Jennifer become a way of life for addicts. Taking drugs or drinking alcohol is a necessary evil to keep from going crazy or being sick with depression. Whatever it takes to get the substances, the addict will do. Traumatic events are ignored or submerged into the person's subconscious, and the ability to feel "normal" or even human is lost. Addicts live in a different world from non-users.

Narcotics Anonymous avows addiction enslaves users, describing them as prisoners of their own minds, condemned by their own guilt. Hope is drowned in a sea of problems and cravings. Attempts to stay clean fail, causing pain and misery. NA helps abusers and non-abusers see that addicts are caught in the grip of their disease, forced to survive any way they can. Confronted with the reality of their addiction, addicts admit they not only manipulated people but also lied, stole, cheated, and some even sold themselves. Cravings forced them to get drugs regardless of the cost or the way.

NA opens addicts' minds to how they justify and rationalize what they did to get the drugs they felt they couldn't live without. Moreover, they explain how addicts suppress or ignore times when they lived in a perpetual nightmare. In short, they help addicts perceive they avoided the reality of their addiction.

Unable to deal with the sense of loss, doom, and degradation, addicts do whatever it takes to survive the vicious cycle in which they are trapped. Unable to admit their addiction, they are hooked and feel hopeless.

CHAPTER 4

THE END AND THE BEGINNING

Sylvia

I'm now averaging 30-40 hydrocodones daily. I wake up sick every morning, feeling like I want to die. I'm terrified to face another day of my miserable life as an addict. But even as I lie in bed shaking, I'm usually thinking desperately about how I can get more pills to make it through the day. My head feels weird and I'm dizzy; I know the pills are killing me, but I don't think I can go one day without them—not to mention the rest of my life.

I am broke, my paycheck from three days ago already squandered on drugs. And now, I'm down to one pill. At six dollars a pill, my paycheck doesn't buy enough to get me through a week, so I steal—from my family, my co-workers, and anyone else who is careless enough to leave money where I can find it, or maybe not careless but trusting that someone will not go through their personal things and steal. With a couple dozen pills dulling my brain, I usually don't worry about getting caught. Sometimes I feel unassailable—no one is going to catch me. Sometimes I hope I get caught so this terrible nightmare will end.

When I woke up on January 6, 2010, like a million other mornings I was worried where I was going to get pills that day and where I was going to get the money to buy them. I didn't have any prescriptions to be filled, so I was going to have to buy them from my dealer and pay a premium price. I was panicky. Even though I had made a deal with God about the withdrawals a few weeks ago (I promised I would quit drugs if He would spare me from withdrawals), I was still worried that they would start any minute. So I gulped down my last pill, knowing one pill was like taking a tic tac but hoping it would be enough to keep the shakes, the stomach cramps, and other withdrawal symptoms from starting. To keep me going until I could get more pills. The promise to God? Maybe I'll try again tomorrow.

I called my dealer on my way to work, but she didn't answer. I didn't panic, because sometimes she just ignored me, as well as other addicts who called, but I was worried. When I arrived, I had to finish taking down Christmas decorations. I had already disassembled the tree downstairs, so I went upstairs to start on the second tree. Although I tried to focus on my work, all I could think about was where I could get money to buy more pills during my lunch break. One of the partners in the firm always had a lot of cash in her purse—I knew because she pulled out her wallet one day to give me money to make a purchase for her. But I also knew because I'd slipped into her office once before and stolen money for pills.

This day I was desperate. I didn't want to steal from the partner, especially from one who had been so nice to me that I felt guilty even thinking about it. But the guilt wasn't as strong as my frantic need for pills, so after I saw her go downstairs, I edged my way into her office when no one was looking. Hurriedly, I grabbed some money out of her wallet without looking to see how much I got. When I slipped into the restroom a few minutes later, I was shocked to pull five hundred dollars out of my pocket. I didn't mean to get that much, but I wasn't going to take it back. Even though I felt horrible for stealing, I was relieved to know I had the money for the pills. Now I just had to find them.

I left a little while later without even calling my dealer—I couldn't go much longer without a pill; she had to have some. When I got to her house, she told me she didn't have any but was supposed to be getting some later that day. My heart sank—just because she said that, it didn't mean she would get them. Her sources were as unstable as her buyers. She had to depend on cocaine addicts to sell her their prescription pain pills to get money to buy illegal drugs. It was a vicious cycle of buying and selling. And cocaine users weren't the most dependable suppliers in the world unless they needed money right away.

I returned to work and at first nothing seemed wrong, but a little while later I noticed people were whispering and closing office doors, like something was going on. I guess I still had enough drugs in me not to worry that I could be the reason. Even when I saw two police officers come in and go upstairs, I still had no idea I had been caught. It wasn't until Ray, the office manager, came to my desk with the officers and asked me to follow them to his office that I thought they might suspect me. I began to get anxious, but thought I could lie my way out of it.

When I first went into Ray's office, one of the cops asked me if I remembered anything about stealing money from someone's office. I tried to look innocent and said, "No." What I didn't know was that because of previous thefts in the partner's office, the firm had installed a video camera there during the Christmas holidays. I had no idea until the police officer rolled the tape.

"Do you remember anything now?" My heart lurching, I said, "I guess I do." There weren't enough pills in me or probably never could be to keep me from being overcome with embarrassment. When the officer told me to turn around so he could handcuff me, I begged him not to because I didn't want my daughter (who was a graphic designer in the same building) to see me walking out that way. Rudely, he told me I should have thought about that earlier. With my head hanging in shame, I stumbled out of the office, handcuffed, as my co-workers stared at me in disbelief. I had walked down that hallway a million times, but that day it was like the Burma Road. When I finally made it to the front desk, I glanced over at the receptionist who I thought had been my friend, but I couldn't read the look on her face. Was it surprise? Or had she known all along and was looking at me with pity? Or maybe it was hate—that I could have betrayed everyone. I really didn't care; I just wanted out the door.

Outside, I was shoved into the police car. The officer asked me where the money was and went back inside to get my purse. With my hands handcuffed behind me, I somehow managed to get my cell phone out of my pocket and dial my sister's number. When she answered, I started telling her I had been arrested for stealing money and was about to be taken to the police station. But the officer came back and I had to stop talking, the phone hidden behind my back. Wretched and distressed, I had wanted my sister to somehow get to my daughter Kacie and make sure she was okay. I was more worried about everybody else at that point than myself. I was getting what I deserved and felt relieved that it was all over. But my daughter didn't deserve this.

At the police station, I was booked, fingerprinted, told what my bond was, and left alone for hours. I had been here before, so I knew it would be a long time before I would see anyone. And it was. I was isolated for about eight hours in a concrete cell. Time crawled by so slowly it was like watching every grain of sand sift through an hourglass; all I could do was sit there and worry about what my family must be going through.

Finally, after Sherry posted my bail, I was released to face her and my two daughters. Kacie was the only one from whom I felt any kind of understanding or forgiveness; Stacie, my older daughter, and Sherry looked at me coldly. They were all sick of my addiction and what it was doing to our family. They had no idea how much I hated myself for what I had put them through. If I had been a selfish person, I would have killed myself that night and not have had to face them again.

But I couldn't leave my kids to grapple with their mother's failure to deal with her life. When I arrived home, though, all I wanted was to get in bed and pull the covers over my head. Like a turtle resting at the bottom of a creek, I wanted to hide from the world. Buried under blankets, I pretended I couldn't feel or hear the horrible comments people were making about me. If they could all just understand how badly I felt about betraying them.... I cried all night and wondered if I could ever get out of that bed.

My guilt plagued me. How many times would I put myself and my kids through this before I had enough sense to stop? How many bottoms would I have to hit before I woke up? Would I ever be able to go on with my life?

Still on probation for stealing money three years previously and having been arrested three weeks earlier on a $500-and-under theft charge for stealing $50 of groceries, I told myself I would never be able to get another job, even if I managed to elude jail time again. Who would hire a 57-year-old addict with multiple felonies?

And how could I be around my kids knowing they thought their mother was a loser drug addict? I had embarrassed them again. Stacie would never trust me again with my grandkids. I knew that my son Bart, who wouldn't talk about my addiction, already thought I was crazy because of all my other arrests. Even worse, Kacie had to go back to work at the same place where I was arrested and face all those people who thought her mother was a worthless, lying thief. I was just sick for all of my kids. I raised three wonderful children to know right from wrong—to not lie, or cheat, or steal. How is it their mother let her mind get so warped she did what she had taught them not to do?

My kids had had a lunatic mother who had been messed up on drugs for 17 years. How could they not hate me? I was sure they did. I hated me.

How did an intelligent person get into a mess like this? Why are drugs and alcohol so powerful they make you do things you would never do without being under their control?

I hoped my kids could somehow remember the mother I used to be—before my addiction.

Kacie

When my mom was arrested at the company where we worked, I was absolutely terrified for her. My first thought wasn't embarrassment or anger. I had never been more worried for her. I hated how scared she was and how ashamed she must feel. I knew that for her to steal money for pills from people she liked and respected at work, she must have hit a drastically low point. It made me incredibly sad.

When they pulled me aside at work to tell me what mom had done, my two initial reactions were worry for her and extreme anger at the company we worked for. I couldn't believe they had arrested her in front of her colleagues, friends, and daughter. The situation could have been dealt with quietly and discreetly. I know what she did was wrong, but in my opinion, how they handled it was just as wrong.

I think people expected me to be embarrassed by what mom had done or angry at her for putting me in that situation at work. I could never feel ashamed of my mom, especially for an addiction that is so difficult to overcome. I could also never feel enraged at her for having a disease that she didn't ask for. But I get mad at the pills themselves. I feel outrage towards pharmaceutical companies, online pharmacies, and doctors who carelessly write prescriptions.

I know my mom is the victim of a truly sad addiction. I could never be embarrassed or angry at her for that.

Sherry

A wintry wind whistled outside the kitchen window in early January as I sat by a warm fire, reading a magazine. When the phone rang, I froze when I heard the panic in the way Sylvia called my name. Even before I heard her distraught words, I knew something was terribly wrong.

"Sherry," she said, terror tinting her words, "I've been arrested." My heart thudding and my stomach churning, I waited for her next words, but she said nothing more.

"Sylvia," I questioned fearfully, "what's happening? Why are you being arrested?" But still Sylvia stayed silent, although I could hear voices in the background. For more than 25 minutes, I paced the floor, cell phone in hand, urging Sylvia to say something, anything, to let me know what was happening. And then the line went dead.

I felt helpless, not even knowing where Sylvia was, unable to go to her. And then Sylvia's daughter Kacie called, telling me her mother had been arrested at the company where they both worked. She told me where the police were taking Sylvia and asked me to meet her there.

I rushed downtown, where both of Sylvia's daughters sat waiting in the stark hallway outside the room at the Criminal Justice Center while their mother was being booked. We briefly hugged, tears clinging to our eyelids. No words were needed—the dismay at knowing Sylvia was in trouble again showed in the slump of our shoulders and our downcast faces.

After sitting silently for a time, we began to talk, wondering how we could have missed the signs again. How could we not have noticed that Sylvia was back on pills? Surely there were warning signals....

In the past, when we gathered like this with fear and panic in our hearts, sometimes anger erupted—furious that Sylvia was putting us through this again. But tonight, instead of rage, compassion for Sylvia's helplessness to combat the power of addiction stifled our selfish thoughts. With deep sadness, we pondered Sylvia's future, dreading the worst and praying for mercy and grace.

Later that night after I had bonded Sylvia out and we returned home, as I sat with her, she sobbed, humiliated at what she had done in a drug-crazed state of mind. Dismayed at the embarrassment she had caused her children. Tormented because she had ruined her life. And most of all, lost and alone because she felt totally and absolutely hopeless.

The long, sleepless night behind us, I arose early and began researching treatment options. Surprisingly, one that popped up in my Internet search was only a few blocks away. Even more unforeseen, in the light of the day, Sylvia brokenly acknowledged she needed help and went willingly to meet with a counselor at Focus Healthcare. In the past, when I and other family members had urged and even pushed Sylvia to get help, she had resisted. And, even when she went for treatment, she didn't want to be there and thus didn't fully benefit from the care she received. But this time, Sylvia's attitude was dramatically different. Before, she had blamed God for her life's problems. Now, she admitted her own responsibility and believed God would help her if she would let him.

Since that day, the change in Sylvia has been nothing short of miraculous. But it was a long, shameful journey that lasted 17 years. One that devastated her financially and bruised her emotionally. One that almost destroyed her health and threatened the love of her children.

Stacie

I am extremely proud of my mom. I have no doubt she has been through *some rough times since she turned her life around, but she has stayed strong and not given in to temptation. Back in control of her mind, she is a resilient woman. I am trying to be able to trust her 100 percent, but it's going to take some time. We are getting along better, and we are closer now—she is a wonderful Nana and mother. I love her—it's good to have her back.*

Kacie

The biggest way my mother's recovery has affected our relationship is that for the first time since I was a teenager, I trust her. I don't feel like I have to analyze her actions all the time or question whether or not she is telling me the truth about something. Because I trust her, I feel much closer to her.

When we are together, I feel like I'm hanging out with my mom, not the fake version who was trying to pretend she hadn't taken pills. When I hear her laugh now, I know it's real and isn't just her trying to pretend to be happy.

This is the first time I've ever really felt like she has beaten her addiction. I know she probably has moments of temptation, but I honestly believe she is strong enough now to never go back to that miserable life. Like Stacie, I'm so glad to have my mom back.

Bart

I'm thankful to have my mom back, too. I have a son now, and it took a while, but my trust has built back enough that I feel safe letting him stay with her. I don't believe she will ever get hooked again. It was hard not to give up when she kept going back to taking drugs, but her addiction had to take its own course and no matter how much we all wanted her to get drug-free, no one could help her until she wanted to help herself. That's what I would tell a friend who had a parent who was addicted: People have to see with their own eyes that drugs make their lives worse, not better. I would also tell them not to give up hope—it may take a long time, but it can happen.

HOW CAN THE ADDICT AVOID GETTING HOOKED AGAIN AND AGAIN?

Clinicians who work with addicts confirm that one or more relapses during ongoing attempts to recover are common and predictable, producing potholes on the road to recovery. For many addicts and their family members, relapse is even more heartrending than the initial substance abuse. Falling back into addiction can be devastating, causing friction in relationships that may already be fragile and frayed.

Susan Merle Gordon, who authored "Relapse & Recovery; Behavioral Strategies for Change," maintains relapse should not be viewed as a failure because it may be an inevitable component of a learning process that leads to lasting recovery. In her research sponsored by the Caron Foundation (one of the nation's oldest and largest addiction treatment centers), Gordon reported that fifty percent of those with addictive diseases relapse into heavy and continuous use and ninety percent relapse for a brief time. Gender is a factor, with women being less likely to relapse than men, partly, Gordon notes, because they are more likely to stay in treatment and participate in group counseling.

The Importance of Aftercare

Experiences in treatment facilities illustrate that aftercare plays a critical role in long-term recovery. In Caron facilities' work with addicts, they have found that more than 60 percent of their patients who regularly attend some type of aftercare following treatment remain substance-free. For patients who attend only sporadically, approximately 40 percent remain abstinent. With those who choose not to participate in aftercare at all, only 30 percent stay drug or alcohol-free.

Relapse is almost guaranteed if a recovering addict falls off his treatment plan, which at Focus Healthcare is recommended to last 3-5 years. Addiction is a disease of relapse, and to avoid relapse, a person is strongly advised to stay in the recovery community.

Aftercare—including groups such as NA, AA, and Celebrate Recovery—provides support and relationships desperately needed for addicts in recovery. These groups serve as lifelines to hope without judgment or criticism. They also help the addict avoid isolation, a precursor to depression and anxiety. Further, if the individual can afford therapy or counseling, he will find help and support in facing issues that have been avoided by using pills or alcohol. Skills can be learned to replace the urge to deal with life's problems through substance abuse.

Dysfunctional relationships rank in the top three reasons for relapse, often because the addict is emotionally dependent. When an addict demands that another person prove his love or expects that person to create an ideal world, tremendous pressure is exerted on the relationship, often making it impossible for the person to live up to the addict's requirements for a happy life. Aftercare, including counseling, assists the addict with emotional immaturity, helping to solve relationship problems.

Learning to Deal with Life

Gordon (2011) notes addiction relapses are not all that different from relapses that occur when patients who have diseases such as diabetes, asthma, and hypertension fail to comply with their treatments. Regardless of the disease, patients must find ways to adjust their lifestyles and assume responsibility for managing their own disease and recovery.

Often, though, the addict is thrown back into life situations he couldn't deal with before and isn't prepared to deal with now. Learning about the genetic and environmental causes of addiction without learning how to face life's problems is not sufficient to protect the addict from relapse. If a person cannot find peace in whatever life he has left after addiction, staying sober becomes a strenuous challenge. Even so, losing a battle two or more times does not mean recovery isn't achievable. An addict who feels he has failed again may think, "I can't go to God with another promise. He has to be disgusted with me for breaking so many commitments. Why would he help me out of another mess of my own making?" Believing he is caught in an endless cycle of recovery and relapse, he thinks he will never make a clean break.

No one is hopeless—even an addict who has relapsed multiple times. As C.S. Lewis declared, "Experience is a brutal teacher, but you learn, by God, you learn." When a person appears to have no hope, she has bypassed a critical step in recovering—acquiring relapse prevention techniques. Learning how to stay sober takes skills—and for some, experience and insight are gained during relapse periods. An addict must learn to depend on something besides alcohol or drugs to deal with her thoughts, feelings, relationships, and behaviors.

The recovery process begins when an addict accepts that his behavior is caused not by circumstances but by his response to those circumstances. Lutzer (1984) says we are all born with a propensity to avoid blame, recalling that Will Rogers once remarked there are two eras in American history—the passing of the buffalo and the passing of the buck! When an addict pleads her case is different, worse than others, she is trying to transfer her blame, the reasons for her actions, to someone else. But Lutzer reminds us that even when "propelled by passions" that appear to be outside a person's control, she still makes a choice. With the choice comes accountability that cannot be shifted to someone else.

Passing the buck takes less emotional energy than admitting responsibility. If someone else is to blame, it is easier to justify staying in the vicious cycle: using alcohol or drugs to escape life's problems; feeling guilty, determining never to do it again; taking pride in brief periods of self-control; then failing one more time. When we repeat this pattern, Lutzer maintains the ruts we cut in our life get deeper, the chains holding us pull tighter.

The choices facing the addict are simple: become more depressed and more defiant, staying in the vicious cycle, or break the chain by coming out of the one-step-forward and two-step-backward dance. Dazed by drugs or alcohol, pulling out of the bitterness and apathy takes a superhuman effort.

John Baker, who created the Celebrate Recovery program to help broken people heal, knew that all human lives are "tangled up with hurts that haunt our hearts, hang-ups that cause us pain, and habits that mess up our lives." Everyone, he says, must face the truth that life isn't easy—it's tough. The world we live in is imperfect. At times, we have been hurt by other people, and we've hurt others. Moreover, we have hurt ourselves. No man or woman walking on earth is perfect; every human being has made mistakes; in short, we've all blown parts of our lives.

Imperfect people in an imperfect world must find a way to survive, and the best hope for doing that is to make choices that heal rather than destroy, that lead to happiness instead of despair, that create peace rather than discord in our hearts and lives. Recovery is possible even though the addict's life will never be perfect, or maybe not even close to what she had hoped it would be. Failures and setbacks can be used as stepping stones to a more meaningful life when she starts making the right choices. Resisting the lure of the bait is where addiction ends and life begins.

A little tugboat was moving down the Mississippi River toward a drawbridge. Although the drawbridge operator was watching as the tug approached and threw the gear to raise the bridge, a malfunction occurred and the bridge failed to open.

The little tugboat saw what was happening and tried to shift gears and back up to avoid hitting the bridge, but the river was running too fast and the tugboat was pulled under the bridge sideways.

Moments passed, and then, from the other side of the bridge, the bridge operator saw the little tugboat's flag. It was low, but it was still flying. As he watched, the tugboat slowly appeared, righting itself.

Addicts may be pulled under, but they can right themselves and continue on life's journey.

PART TWO

Patterns of Addiction

CHAPTER 5

VULNERABILITY

We are all vulnerable to addiction of one kind or another: food, caffeine, tobacco, Internet shopping, cars, video games, social networking web sites like Facebook, gambling, work, or numerous other items or activities for which we develop compulsions or obsessions. Yet, not everyone gets hooked. Some people play the lottery only occasionally, while others get so addicted they use money needed for groceries and rent to play the games. Some can only smoke one cigarette after dinner, but others can't survive without three packs a day. One person loves decadent desserts but stops indulging herself before becoming overweight; yet many can't stop eating their way into obesity. A young mother makes an occasional Internet purchase, but a friend spends her entire day every day searching for antique clocks and watches—even though her home and garage are already filled with similar items from previous purchases, and her credit card debt mounts to tens of thousands of dollars.

The possibilities for addiction are unlimited, yet, despite the diversity, the substances that immediately come to mind when the word "addict" is used are alcohol and legal/illegal drugs. Many years ago, we pictured an addict as some unlucky soul who had a poor upbringing—a person without a family, usually homeless. The addict certainly wasn't someone who looked like we do, a co-worker, or one of our family members. He didn't sit next to us in the church pew or own the local franchise for highly profitable optical stores. The addict looked and dressed differently, often appearing deranged, unable to function in society. Today, the secret is out. The picture of the addict has changed, and she looks as normal as we do.

Washton and Boundy (1989) describe the breadth of the problem: "This epidemic of compulsive behaviors is not just happening in urban ghettos, or to poor people, the uneducated, or to one particular race. It's happening in every small town and big city in America; behind the doors of sprawling mansions, suburban track houses, and high-rise apartments alike; among the highly educated as well as those barely out of grade school; among people of all colors and all classes. We don't have to look any farther than our own hometown, our own block, and often even our own family to find stories of addiction and the pain it carves into people's lives."

What is it within human beings that makes people in such varied walks of life vulnerable to being hooked by poisonous bait?

As she talks about susceptibility, Monteleone avows, "Genetics load the gun, and environment pulls the trigger." In addition to neutron pathways predisposed to rerouting by alcohol or drugs, Monteleone notes many addicts come from home environments that failed to help develop emotional, intellectual, and social skills. Functional families assist children in developing these competencies, while dysfunctional families leave children with a deficit of skills that help them navigate problems in acceptable ways. According to Monteleone, "Treatment thus becomes a skill-building process," helping people learn how to steer away from the shoals of life and find safe waters for moving forward. "The skill development occurs without the addict being made to feel shame or guilt. In essence, the addict is able to see the truth of his or her life without judgment. The goal is to help people live in a community with dignity and respect while facing and dealing with addiction."

Today, we grow up and live in an obsessive/compulsive society surrounded by situations that generate vulnerability to addiction. We want instant happiness, money, and perfect love. We want what we see on television and the Internet—glamorous clothes, shapely bodies, handsome houses. Our needs and wants consume us, and uncontrollable desires can overtake us if we create an idyllic self or life that is not attainable. Under such conditions, what tempts one person into addiction while another resists is more than just genetic makeup, and it is not just where we live and the people with whom we associate; not just our ethnicity or our status in life. We are vulnerable not because of what we are or are not on the outside; we are vulnerable because of who we are inside.

Our identity as a person comes from how we see ourselves. The first lines on the canvas of our self-portrait are drawn during childhood, and as we grow and develop, colors and shapes are added, some vibrant and distinctive, others sharp-edged and dark. We form deep-rooted opinions about our capabilities—as well as our flaws and imperfections.

Terry C, a Chattanooga artist, constantly created whimsical artwork in his childhood. As he entered his teenage years, he says he began to doubt the worth of his creative vision. "I began to tell myself I was wasting time painting and drawing...so I just quit." His self-image no longer measuring up to his ideal for creativity, Terry abandoned his passion and attempted to fill his emptiness with alcohol and drugs. The path he chose led to crime and homeless life on the streets, where he almost died in 1989. In hindsight, he wonders if his addiction was hereditary. His grandfather was an alcoholic, although he hid it well. Even so, his grandfather told family members when Terry was 10 or 11-years old: "I'm worried about Terry. He's like me."

Thankfully, like his grandfather, Terry finally dislodged the hook. Today, he is a well-known and highly respected artist. The transformation came after a near-death experience, from which he gained a spiritual awareness, leading to his reunion with his creative expression. But before that happened, he had to rebuild his self-image—he had to believe in himself and his talent again.

In the end, we become the composite of our life experiences, small and large, good and bad, and they affect not only how we see ourselves but also how we perceive the world and our place in it. These views in turn influence our feelings, our behaviors, and our personality.

BELIEF SYSTEMS

Within our inner being lies a belief system—values, ideas, and principles that become our compass. These deeply held core beliefs, McKay and Fanning (1991) tell us, are the bedrock of personalities. "They describe you as worthy or worthless, competent or incompetent, powerful or powerless, loved or scorned, self-reliant or dependent, belonging or outcast, trusting or suspicious, judgmental or accepting, secure or threatened, fairly treated or victimized." When we choose the negative of each of the contrasting descriptors, we define ourselves as less worthy than others, casting the vulnerability hook into the water.

In a family environment where messages intentionally or unintentionally convey unachievable benchmarks, beliefs are translated into "should's" that contribute to susceptibility to addiction:

- I should be a better person (or better mother, or better son, or better____).

- I should have my needs met.
- I should be happy.
- I should be able to make others happy.
- I should be smarter.
- I should have everything everyone else has.
- I should have a more worthwhile purpose for my life.
- I should be perfect.
- I should be in control not only of myself but also of others.
- I should not have to live with pain—emotional or physical.
- I should be able to find the answers to my problems outside myself.

Monteleone's list is shorter. She avows there are four core beliefs every addict must tackle and conquer:

1 – I'm a bad and unworthy person. (This creates toxic shame.)

2 – I'm not loveable as I am.

3 – If I depend on someone else to get my needs met, they'll never get met.

4 – Alcohol (or drugs, money, food, or sex) is my most important need.

Both the longer and shorter lists reflect how the person sees himself and his needs—unable to measure up to an idealized picture of himself and his life. He "should," but he "can't." When a person is unable to fulfill (check off) one or more of his "should's," his self-image deteriorates. Feeling powerless over his life, he seeks an escape from his feelings or his problems.

It must be noted that the potential addict doesn't necessarily go looking for drugs or alcohol as a way out. Many times she discovers by accident that pills given for a headache, a throbbing tooth, pain following surgery, or injuries from a car accident produce a sense of well-being that masks not only pain but also emotional problems, at least temporarily. The euphoria from the first pills is attractive, and she seeks to re-find the feeling of contentment that has so long eluded her.

FAMILY SECRETS
Family relationships often contribute to vulnerability to addiction. In

families where parents are not there emotionally for their children, unmet dependency needs can carry over into adulthood. When emotions cannot be freely and honestly expressed, they bottle up, often resulting in a feeling of rejection. If the situation includes physical or emotional abuse, the threatening environment can leave the child feeling wounded and abandoned; shame sometimes twists into guilt, adding the burden of self-recrimination.

Gary A, a recovering addict who served 15 years as an addiction counselor, declares the biggest problem in dealing with addicts and their families is the secret door behind which many abuse stories reside. He tells of Cindy, whose mother died when she was 10. In the mountains of Kentucky, hidden from others, Cindy's dad started sexually abusing her two years later. Unable to deal with the humiliation and guilt, Cindy began cutting herself. Physical pain kept her from thinking about the emotional hurts; and, compared to the agony of her mind, the cuts weren't all that bad. When her school noted the tell-tale signs of self-mutilation and drugs, Cindy ended up in Tennessee for treatment. Her father encouraged her to go, telling her he wanted her to get better. He urged Cindy to tell counselors everything—except "about us."

After detox, without the influence of drugs to drag her conscience into oblivion, Cindy told all. Confronted by Gary when he came to the treatment center for family week, Cindy's father admitted he had abused his daughter. Shamefaced and shaken, he also disclosed he himself had been abused by an uncle. Abuse left both Cindy and her father vulnerable to addiction—escape from their pain-ridden emotions came from prescription drugs when they separately found that lows from downers camouflaged hurts, and highs from uppers offered new-found exhilaration. Only after facing their deep-seated issues was healing possible.

In another case coming from the same Kentucky addiction council that referred Cindy, a 16-year-old young man named Logan had taken the brunt of his father's distress after his mother had abruptly left two years previously. As in Cindy's case, it eventually came out that the father himself had been abused (this time physically), telling terrible tales of his own dad chaining him to a newel post to beat him. Counseling helped Logan and his father work through their damaged emotions, leading them to understand that drugs were a temporary solution, not the cure for their hurts.

From years of experience, Gary proclaims, "It is not enough to deal with just the collateral problems of addiction—the core problem, often dark secrets, must be brought into the open and dealt with before the addict can recover." As long as false pictures are presented to the outside world, the inner problems will continue to create vulnerability and drug use can ensue.

Fear, insecurity, and a negative self-image are fertile breeding grounds for addiction.

CHAPTER 6

ADDICTIVE PERSONALITY TRAITS

a sense that image is everything frequently underlies an addictive personality. Today's society creates the false impression that we can be everything and have everything, where technology enables us to continuously compare ourselves and our possessions to idealized pictures. If our self-image is based on other people, their abilities, looks, possessions, friends, and success, having what they have and being like them is requisite to feeling good about ourselves. We want more, think we need more, and feel compelled to get more—the self-imposed pressure for more becomes a disease in our heads.

INABILITY TO DELAY GRATIFICATION

Most people can deal with getting what they need or want over a period of time, as resources are available. In contrast, the addictive personality is impatient or unwilling to delay gratification. A desire for loving parents or a loving spouse, a need for financial or physical security, a compulsion to escape emotional problems—all push a person to find satisfaction, solutions, or a way out. For an addict, drugs seem the easiest, most effortless path.

Concerns may arise from a dysfunctional family, an intolerable work situation, a failure to communicate, or countless other matters; while the pressure may be a matter of degree, the impulse to avoid the real issue is the driving force behind addiction. When faced with problems, quick fixes are sought to meet needs and wants. Often, the person's belief system has created a sense of entitlement: "I deserve more than I have." "I see others who didn't have to work for what they want; why should I?" "The world has mistreated me—it owes me." "If I can't get what I want and need, there must be something wrong with me."

Sam was married to Tanya, who had a twin sister. The twin sister's husband was a successful surgeon who provided a castle-like house for his wife and two children, took them on European trips, and sent his children to private schools. Sam, a college graduate, had only moderate success as an insurance agent, and he and Tanya didn't manage their limited resources well so they were always in debt. The root of the problem was that they wanted to live the same "good life" that Tanya's twin and her husband did. They bought a house they couldn't afford, dressed in expensive clothes purchased with overloaded credit cards, enrolled their three girls in private schools, and spent money as if they would someday find a pot of gold at the end of a rainbow. When the bills mounted so high they couldn't keep up, Tanya berated Sam because he didn't measure up to her sister's husband. Ashamed and disgraced by a foreclosure notice that followed on the heels of bill collectors for credit cards, Sam drowned his sorrows in liquor. Finding relief, he was hooked.

EMOTIONAL ISSUES

Human beings have an innate drive to find happiness and peace. Most of us achieve these feelings at times in our life, bringing a sense of completeness. But then, the sense of peace and beauty slips away, almost always to return another time.

The natural cycle of positive and negative emotions is not a sequence we can control. We can either accept the rotations or resist them. Fighting only leads to frustration—no one is happy and content 100 percent of the time. When we fail to accept the shifting sands of good and bad times, we may panic that our lives will never be "good" or "normal" again. The temptation to run away from problems or escape sadness can cause us to withdraw, feeling sorry for ourselves as we mourn the pitiful state of our lives.

An addictive personality sometimes stems from such a sense of isolation. Wrestling with unmet desires, needs, and problems alone, the person may feel abandoned, even if her exile is self-imposed. Carol, a divorced mother with three children, had no one to whom she could turn for help. Faced with financial issues, routine household responsibilities, and behavioral problems with her children, she felt totally cut off from a world where most women had husbands who met (or at least helped meet) their needs. Self-conscious and ashamed that she couldn't provide for her children, she became more and more stressed, resulting in panic attacks. When her doctor prescribed anti-anxiety medication, she found a stabilizing force for her emotions and was relieved she no longer awakened scared to face the day. Soon, she became dependent on the pills to avoid anxiety attacks during the day. Then, she needed the drugs to be less nervous as she got her quarreling children ready for school. Day by day, it took increasingly more pills to get through the waking hours and sleepless nights. She was hooked.

Fragile emotions contribute to an addictive personality. Scarred from life experiences, either in childhood or adulthood, the addict dons armor for protection. Desperate for approval from others, he is shaken by perceived slights and criticisms that penetrate the shield, which is never quite thick enough to protect him.

Doug grew up with a demanding mother who had little patience with a growing boy's antics. Expecting exemplary performance in school, she chastened him when he didn't measure up to her standards for studying. If his report card was less than perfect, she didn't hesitate to let him know she was hurtfully disappointed. No matter how hard he tried, Doug was never good enough to win his mother's approval. Early on, he learned her love was conditioned on living up to her romanticized image of what a son should be. When friends at a party offered 12-year-old Doug drugs to lift his spirits, he took the bait. Soon, he was scavenging his mother's medicine cabinet for her prescription bottles. He was hooked.

Later, in the workplace, Doug's learned fear of disapproval and rejection made him interpret constructive criticism as belittlement. If someone questioned him about a decision, he took it personally, sometimes attacking the messenger. But inside, he disparaged himself for not being good enough to avoid negative comments. By now, he had his own prescriptions, and when they weren't sufficient, he started using the Internet to order the pills he craved. When that source evaporated, he didn't have any trouble finding a dealer on the street. For a while, the more he took, the better he felt about himself. But then the opposite effect morphed him into a walking zombie. He did not know, or perhaps he just didn't care, that his co-workers and family knew—he was hooked.

Children and adults alike learn to expect rejection when they are repeatedly made to feel they cannot be good enough or work hard enough to earn approval. Taught that what other people think is of supreme importance, they become overly concerned with their image.

Tom's mother hammered into his brain that he must, at all costs, protect the family name. Even as an adult, Tom worried about what other people thought. After a small business in which he had heavily invested failed, he was mortified. When the bankruptcy was reported in a local newspaper and his name made the nightly news, he was filled with shame and guilt. That night, he stopped by a local bar and had a few beers to dull his disappointment in himself. The next night, he did the same thing. Even when he found a new job, he continued to drink to deaden his fear of losing another job. At first, it was only in the evening when he was alone with his anxiety. But when his nightmares replayed his devastating misfortune, the mornings found him shaken and apprehensive. Soon, he was drinking several beers before he went to work to ward off fears of failure and rejection. Then it took a few more drinks to face the afternoon. He was hooked.

Emotional numbness often follows repeated hurts, failures, or disappointments. To protect herself after divorce from an abusive husband, Jane shelved her damaged feelings in a secret place in her mind, refusing to think about them. Instead of seeking help, she withdrew into a shell, accepting without protest whatever the world put on her. Occasionally, Jane filled the void with frenzied activity, cleaning her house from top to bottom or baking more cakes than she could ever give away—as long as she was occupied, she didn't have to face how she felt about herself. But when the activity ended, her numbness returned. When her friends offered her drugs they said would make her feel better, she thought, "Why not?" Tired of feeling barren inside, she jumped at the possibility of feeling full of life again. For the first time in years, her emotional lows turned into highs of excitement and ecstasy. She felt alive. It was a feeling she wanted to repeat—and she did. She was hooked.

John Greenleaf Whittier reminds us, "For all sad words of tongue or pen, the saddest are these: 'It might have been.'" When we continue to cast emotional issues out as lures into a sea of drugs or alcohol, we look backward, trying to drown hurts and regrets. If only the hurts hadn't happened; if only the hook hadn't seemed like the solution for getting out of the churning waters, it might have been different.

Lutzer proclaims we can't obscure our past—we must deal with it before we can experience freedom in the future, noting that what "troubles you today sank its roots into your life yesterday." What's past is past, and it can never be erased, but an addict cannot let it shape his future. Shame must be worked through and then abandoned, or illegitimate use of guilt will only multiply discouragement and susceptibility.

CHAPTER 7

DESTRUCTIVE BEHAVIORS
OF ADDICTIVE PERSONALITIES

GUILT AND SHAME

Of all the characteristics of addictive personalities, guilt and shame are often the most destructive. A long-term and overriding guilt complex, complicated by self-reproach, creates a formidable force that pulls a person down into a dark chasm. Dragged through the murky waters of a depressed mind, troubled thoughts may cause continuous replays of past actions, reinforcing self-perpetuating expectations of failure. Even when an addict can suppress the internalized blame, dark moods and depressive states of mind take their toll.

Living with guilt is a heavy burden. It is like trying to get a car out of a snow bank. No matter how much gas the addict gives the car, her wheels just continue to spin. The slick ruts from the spinning are coated with her shame, and she thinks she will be stuck there for the rest of her life.

Unresolved guilt drags a person's spirit into the cold snow, creating ice in the heart that can't be melted. It's easier to give up than to try to thaw frozen feelings of worthlessness and deal with them. The addict knows he has "blown it," and he sees no way to go back and undo the damage. "I might as well give up. I'm a bad person and that isn't going to change." Filled with humiliation, he doesn't want to try again. This willingness to give up is typical of addictive personalities.

Guilt and shame are like chains that keep a person locked into past behaviors and failures. Some people salve their consciences, justifying their actions with irrational rationalizations: "I would never have done what I did if Sammy hadn't left me." "I wouldn't have stolen if my mother had given me cash when I asked for it." "The company has so much money no one will ever miss what I took." "I need the dress to make me feel better about myself." "I wouldn't have struck back in anger if he hadn't provoked me." Sometimes the convoluted thoughts are based on blaming others, but they may also arise from the need to build self-image. The end result is the same: a guilt trip.

Addictive teenagers and senior citizens alike, and everyone in between, fight their feelings with substances that offer relief, often beginning innocently only to accidentally discover a way to mask guilt and shame from life's hurts and behaviors. Medication for back pain, sedatives for sleep, anxiety medicine for nervousness—seemingly harmless beginnings that provide respite far beyond the physical ailment. And when the desire for drugs becomes a craving, the person is hooked.

Guilt and shame pack a double whammy. They are often precursors to addiction when a person seeks to escape feeling bad about himself. On the other end of the continuum, guilt and shame return with vengeance after inappropriate behavior and actions occur while the person is under the influence of mind-altering drugs or alcohol. Feeling uninhibited and invincible because of the chemical changes, the person may steal—from family members, co-workers, or strangers. With a conscience lulled by heavy doses of medication, the addict thinks he deserves what he takes. The world isn't fair, or he would have as much as others have.

Sometimes she needs what she takes, sometimes she just steals because it makes her feel powerful, and sometimes she is desperate for money to support her habit. Regardless of the reason, when the mind-altering effects of drugs or alcohol wear off, guilt and shame fill the empty space. As Washton and Boundy note, the cycle self-perpetuates. The greater the guilt, the bigger the need for relief in drugs; the more drugs ingested, the greater the guilt; and on and on the crazy cycle goes. Sylvia experienced this vicious cycle as she repeatedly stole—sometimes money and for a while, prescription pads—to get the medication she desperately needed to make her brave enough to do what she had to do to procure the pills. When she could silence her shame and guilt, she could do the unthinkable that violated her moral belief system. Even the potential consequences became covered in her conscious mind, concealed by the effect of the drugs.

INADEQUATE COPING SKILLS

At the root of Sylvia's actions causing remorse was an inability to cope with life's problems and stressors. The youngest child, she was only five years old when she discovered her mother unconscious, felled by a stroke. That night, as her mother lay in the hospital, Sylvia cried and wrung her hands, whimpering: "Mama, daddy, mama, daddy." In acute distress, she uttered the frightened cries over and over as her father held her in his arms, walking back and forth, attempting to soothe and calm her, but she was shaken beyond comfort. From that day forward, Sylvia was often nervous and fearful about life—worried about what might happen. In an effort to help, family members often indulged her, and her sister Sherry became the primary caregiver during her school years after her father became too ill to help and her mother was busy caring for him. During this critical time in her life, Sylvia failed to develop the tools to deal with the cards life held in store for her.

People who are victims of others' compulsions to solve their problems don't develop coping mechanisms. They fail to pause and analyze the problem from all angles in order to develop and evaluate options before taking decisive action. In many cases, they have not learned to tolerate uncertainty, annoyances, or disappointments. If they were raised in an overly critical family, they may be too hard on themselves. On the other hand, the person may be self-centered, unwilling to cooperate or negotiate. The lack of communication skills—the ability to express feelings or thoughts without offending others—can also contribute to the failure to solve problems effectively.

In the absence of adequate coping skills, an addictive personality seeks escape from his problems. Medication and alcohol can lull him into thinking he doesn't need to worry about his dilemmas—or at least enable him to get away from them for fleeting periods of time. Unfortunately, ignoring problems often makes them worse. And, the drugs or alcohol create a whole new realm of difficulties.

The Blame Game

These new problems can generate another set of behaviors typical of addiction: Blaming others. Blaming the past. Blaming fears and weaknesses. Blaming family members. It becomes a game—a blame game. The person works diligently to hold someone else responsible for her bad behaviors, her addiction, or her predicaments. When responsibility is shifted, there is little hope the person will seek ways to constructively address his issues. Moreover, if a person doesn't feel accountable for his actions and problems, he has surrendered his power for solving them to others. Conversely, because much of life is a self-fulfilling prophecy, if an addict believes he can save himself, he can. Like the crafty mule in an old parable, sometimes a person has to take responsibility for himself instead of waiting on the world to solve his problems.

The story tells about a farmer whose old mule fell into a well. Looking down, the farmer could hear the mule braying (or was he praying?) and felt sorry for him. Deciding the mule couldn't be saved, the man started shoveling dirt in to bury the mule to put it out of its misery. At first, the old mule was hysterical, braying louder and louder. But after a while, the farmer didn't hear anything and thought he had covered the mule. To be sure, though, he kept shoveling in more dirt. What the farmer didn't know is that the old mule had decided to "shake it off and step up"—every time a shovel load of dirt landed on his back, he shook it off and stepped on top of it. This he did repeatedly, as blow after blow of dirt hit his back. No matter how heavy the load or how distressing the situation seemed, the old mule fought panic and just kept right on shaking it off and stepping up. It wasn't long before the mule, filthy and exhausted, successfully stepped over the wall of the well—to the astonishment of the farmer.

The moral of the story—something that could bury a person may actually help save him. Like the mule, if an addict accepts responsibility for his problems, refuses to give in to panic or self-pity, he will be open to positive ways to use the problems in ways that can benefit him. In any seemingly hopeless situation, there is always a way out.

Part of the NA and AA strategy is to take inventory of past mistakes and accept ownership of them, because giving up the victim stance is requisite for recovery.

The third time Sylvia was in rehabilitation treatment, she wrote: *I've lost track of how many jobs I have lost thru the years—probably around 15. I always blamed my terminations on someone else, but I'm sure they all had something to do with drugs. Maybe God was trying to get my attention with each firing and I just didn't listen. How could anybody be so stupid? How many times does a person have to hit bottom before she wakes up? In my case it's been so many times I've lost count.*

Drugs [and alcohol] are a horrible thing. They can ruin a person's life, and you don't even know it is happening. They cause you to do things you wouldn't have done without them. They alter your thinking. They make people hate you. The only friends I have now are my old high school friends I reconnected with on Facebook, because the Sylvia they remember was a good, honest person. Every friend during my years of addiction has somehow been affected by my drug use. I either stole from them or they heard about my stealing from someone else. I had become a stranger—even to myself.

Drugs make you have zero confidence in yourself, yet while you are using them you feel powerful. They make you want more and more. They make you think you don't need God or that God doesn't want anything to do with you while you're using. They are more important to you than God, because they make you feel they have taken your problems away—with God it's in His time and you don't want to wait. And that's if He cares at all. Your head is so messed up each time you use you think maybe He's the cause of all your problems. Punishing you for something you did or didn't do.

You think the drugs are getting rid of your mental pain and guilt, but they are causing it. That's why they are so powerful. They make you think the world owes you something, so it is easy to blame everyone else for anything bad in your life.

In retrospect, Sylvia sees how she shifted responsibility—and blame—for bad things that happened to her. But at the time, pointing the finger at others kept her from feeling worse about herself than she already did. Dependency patterns from childhood contributed to her need for others to be held accountable for her actions, creating an addictive personality susceptible to being hooked by the lure of "feel better" drugs.

False Sense of Security

Addiction offers false security and safety to the dependent personality who allows someone else to take care of him. Later, in the absence of the security blanket, if he feels sad and lonely, an "upper" can pick him up and make him happy. If he can't face that he screwed up his life, a downer calms his fears and anxiety. If the emotional pain from abuse is too distressing, drugs or alcohol can make him forget. If the boss is too hard on him, a few drinks will relieve the stress. In the escape, the addictive personality begins to operate outside the boundaries of society. He says and does things he would never say or do if not under the influence of drugs or alcohol.

Today, Sylvia says, *All of this seems like a dream to me as I look back. I can't imagine trying or even wanting to steal anything now. I thought stealing and failing had become my way of life and that was the kind of person I was. The drugs had such an unshakeable grip on me, I couldn't see a way out to be the person I once was. Even worse, I couldn't even remember who I used to be.*

For me, courage for getting unhooked from drugs was like having faith to cross an old, shaky, broken-down bridge. I didn't want to start because I was terrified I would fall off. Even when I had the guts to get going, I wanted to back off the bridge, returning to what I mistakenly thought was safety. But as I began to go farther, I started to gain confidence that I might make it, and I wasn't so scared. When I saw real safety—my well-

being— ahead on the other side of the bridge, I felt hopeful and was glad I hadn't turned around. When I finally made it to the end, I grasped that God had been there waiting the whole time—that he had been watching me and wasn't going to let me fall. And, as long as I continue to believe and walk in faith, he never will.

Displaced Anger

Another form of destructive behavior typical of addiction is anger. When dealing with an addictive personality, it is critical to understand that anger falling like hail doesn't tell the whole story. There are always currents and temperatures in the clouds that cause the hail to form before it is unleashed on unsuspecting people who may be in the wrong place at the wrong time. Filled with pain and shame, the person lets go against an easy target he knows will not fight back. He may not even realize he is transferring internal rage—his anger against himself for whatever he has done—to others.

To avoid ambushing other people with anger, the addict has to admit his own pain is so severe his twisted mind is pushing him to inflict injury on others in an attempt to heal his own hurt. Sometimes it is not easy to hear the cry behind the seething storm of wrath. Externally, an addict may exude self-righteousness and strong will, but beneath the veneer reside hurt, loneliness, insecurity, and fear. When these emotions make their way to the surface, displaced fury flies in unexpected and often unfair paths.

Buddy hated his parents; he hated his teachers; he hated the whole world. No one gave him any respect, and he convinced himself he didn't care. On the surface, he was cocky and self-assured, but underneath he was paddling furiously. Strict rules at home infuriated him, and he refused to comply. When his parents threatened to take his car, he grabbed the keys and took off so fast he went into a tailspin. He could make it on his own; everyone needed to stay out of his way. A drug habit that had begun with stealing a few Vicidin pills from his parents' medicine cabinet escalated into a risky combination of prescription painkillers and alcohol. Buddy soon found himself fighting with other kids on the street, not realizing he was attacking them—transferring his anger—for what he considered his parents' mistreatment of him. It wasn't long before he joined a gang. He was hooked—on drugs and on violence.

Like many angry, confused teens, Buddy turned to prescription drugs because they were readily available either at home or at a party. A January 2008 report from the Office of the National Drug Control Policy reported that 70 percent of teens who abuse prescription pain relievers say they got them from friends or relatives. Pent-up anger finds an easy outlet when drugs are so readily available.

Anger is not always bad—it can be both healthy and unhealthy. A stress reliever if handled appropriately, anger can alleviate problems if it brings real reasons for disagreement to the surface. But if the rage is an emotional response rather than a rational one, it can be damaging, especially if the anger is misdirected. Unfortunately, those who have not learned to handle emotions constructively get caught in an anger trap. Carter (2003) describes their rage as raw, ready to be rubbed the wrong way even when the target is not the source of the offense. Chained by guilt, distrust, shame, insecurity, or pseudo egotism, the person uses anger to anesthetize his negative self-image, hurting people she loves and sabotaging relationships.

Displaced anger says, "I don't care what you think or how you feel." The world is the enemy, and whoever is closest gets caught in the crossfire. What the person doesn't realize is that today's anger is releasing pent-up feelings, often criticism, condemnation, or rebellion. Anger arises, Carter says, from the painful discovery that love isn't unconditional and thus rejection is possible. Under the influence of drugs or alcohol, the inflamed emotions demand attention, and the addict seeks relief from pain by attacking others. Fragile, tender feelings cause the person to overreact to small slights, unfriendly associates, rude drivers, and others who may not mean anything personal. The "chip on the shoulder" syndrome is uncontrollable.

The underlying cause of anger may stem from an abusive childhood, a sense of abandonment, an unsuccessful attempt to hold feelings inside, or numerous other situations, but in all cases, mood-altering chemicals can cause simmering rage to boil over. Potter-Efron (2007) offers an analogy to describe what happens when anger is allowed to build without release: He describes an emotional container—filled with our strong emotions, in this case rage—that humans carry around. The container doesn't have rigid sides, though; in fact, it's more like a balloon that contracts when not filled with emotions. When we get mad or sad or whatever, the balloon expands. Potter-Efron goes on to say that some people are fortunate enough to have balloons that expand very easily, but most balloons have limits to their expandability. The balloon's skin gets thinner and thinner as emotions continue to pour in, and at some point, the balloon inevitably bursts. When the walls of a balloon are affected by chemicals (drugs or alcohol), the stretching point is diminished, wreaking havoc on self as well as others.

Inability to control anger and unwillingness to take responsibility create an explosive combination in a personality already fraught with insecurity and fear. Destructive behavior ensues.

THE CONTINUUM OF PSYCHOLOGICAL CHARACTERISTICS

The National Academy of Sciences, in a study that brought together much of the existing research on the role of personality in addiction, concluded that no one set of psychological characteristics covers all addictions. However, the report identifies a number of factors that set a person up to vulnerability to addiction:

- A sense of social alienation

- A general tolerance for deviance

- A sense of heightened stress

- A tendency toward impulsive behavior

- An inability to delay gratification

- An antisocial personality

- A disposition toward sensation seeking

- A high value on nonconformity combined with a weak commitment to the goals for achievement valued by the society

When we read this list and look at the preceding sections on addictive personalities, we can all see some of ourselves. Many of the characteristics, traits, and behaviors can be found in each of us—we are all somewhere on the continuum, and we all seek ways to alleviate emotional or physical pain. But for some, when they seek safe harbor in the first drink or pill, genetics kick in and the fish is hooked.

CHAPTER 8

ENABLERS & CO-DEPENDENTS

We want to "fix" someone we love if we think he is broken. When he doesn't control his addiction, we try to do it for him. Good reasons abound: Protect the family name. Avoid embarrassment. Keep the person out of jail. And sometimes, we continue to help because everyone else has given up on him. "If I don't help, something bad will happen to him." We often feel that, without our help, the addict will fail or even die from overdose or suicide.

THE SYNDROME OF HELPING

The terms "co-dependents" and "enablers" are often interchangeably, and they do have similar behaviors, including assuming responsibility for the addict's actions. However, in most cases, the co-dependent's deeds are based both on helping the addict and self-survival, while enablers are motivated almost solely by a desire to avoid bad consequences for the addict. Within this distinction, the terms are both used in the discussion that follows the section on characteristics of co-dependence.

CHARACTERISTICS OF CO-DEPENDENCE

The Council on Co-Dependents Anonymous (CODA) has identified five patterns of co-dependence characteristics, all also applicable to enabling. Within these categories, behaviors can be recognized. A few examples follow:

Denial

- Minimizing how you feel

- Perceiving yourself as completely unselfish and dedicated to the well-being of others
- Labeling others with your own negative traits
- Expressing negativity or aggression in indirect and passive ways

Low Self-Esteem
- Judging what you say, think, or do as never good enough
- Being embarrassed when you receive recognition or compliments
- Having difficulty admitting you make mistakes
- Being unable to ask others to help meet your needs
- Needing to always be right

Compliance
- Being exceptionally loyal
- Putting aside your own interests in order to do what others want
- Being vigilant at protecting the feelings of others

Control
- Believing most people are incapable of taking care of themselves
- Attempting to convince others what to think, do, or feel
- Offering advice and direction to others without being asked
- Using terms of recovery to control the addict

Avoidance
- Judging harshly what others think, say, or do
- Using indirect and evasive communication to avoid confrontation or conflict
- Suppressing your own feelings or needs
- Acting in ways that encourage others to reject, shame, or express anger toward you

A complete list of CODA's "Patterns and Characteristics of Codependence" may be found at http://www.coda.org/tools4recovery/patterns-new.htm.

PATTERNS OF CO-DEPENDENCY AND ENABLING

The basis of co-dependency is not, as many people assume, a desire to control as much as it is a need to be controlled by others. When this need results in an inability to say "no" or stand up for themselves, co-dependents end up victims in physically or emotionally abusive relationships. They confuse being needed with being loved, letting the addict manipulate them, acquiescing to demands, becoming the brunt of misdirected anger or other behaviors. The co-dependent finds it is easier to give in than to stand firm and take the consequences.

If the addict becomes angry, the co-dependent berates herself, "If I had not moved the furniture (or cleaned the garage, or driven the car, or burned the food, or made him angry, or questioned where he had been), he would not have hit me (or yelled at me, or been hateful to the kids, or gotten into an argument at work, or started drinking again)." With this rationalization, the co-dependent assumes responsibility for the addict's actions. The co-dependent's thought process involves self-blame—"If I can be good enough, or loving enough, I can change the addict's behavior; and if I can't, I am to blame and must help the person avoid the consequences of his actions."

In contrast to the co-dependent, the enabler often has a need to control, relating to others by taking care of them. In addition, she is strongly motivated to take responsibility for the addict's actions because she can't bear the thoughts of the consequences to the addict if she doesn't.

Compelled by this strong sense of responsibility for the other person, the enabler attempts to influence the self-destructive behavior. Believing he is more capable than others, the enabler provides "suggestions" or instructions to the addict and often fulfills tasks for her. These thinly disguised efforts to encourage the addict to act in certain ways are resented and dismissed by the addict.

Even in the face of resentment, the enabler not only gives advice, he also gives time, emotion, money, and other resources to the addict in a loving desire to "fix" the person and protect him from bad consequences. Typically, the enabler has a difficult time denying the addict any request. Even when previous efforts have failed and the enabler attempts to show "tough love," trying to force the addict to change, with enough emotional pressure from the addict, the enabler caves and does whatever the addict wants.

The enabler eventually becomes obsessed with rescuing the addict. In the process, the addict learns he does not have to face the consequences of his actions—he knows his enabler will always come through, that she will pick up the pieces if the addict cries long enough and hard enough.

At some point, if the behavior does not change, the enabler becomes addicted to enabling the addict, becoming obsessively involved in the addict's problems. Other aspects of the enablers' life move to second place, often damaging relationships with family members who may not only feel abandoned but also see the enabler as doing more harm than good.

ENDING CO-DEPENDENCY AND ENABLING

Like other addictions, co-dependency and enabling are progressive, becoming worse if not addressed. Monteleone recommends treatment for people who can't say no to an addict. "Addiction is a disease of regression," she says. "The addict struggles with an addictive substance. The enabler is addicted to fixing the person, trying to control the person's actions. In some cases, the co-dependent becomes compulsive and obsessed with the patient's recovery, neglecting his own life and relationships. Addiction within families creates a parallel process—everyone goes down, and the patient becomes more and more addicted."

We become trapped in a vicious cycle, where our efforts to help only prolong the addiction, which in turn results in more destructive actions requiring another rescue. Like one bumper car chasing another in a carnival ride, collisions are inevitable. And, when the ride starts again, even though you may cruise along for a while without crashing, you can be certain another collision waits around the next curve.

In some cases, even enablers give up on an addict, no longer trusting them or giving up hope. Monteleone explains that the person without trust has probably suffered at the hand of the addict—emotionally, physically, or financially. "The addict has to learn to accept reality—that the family needs time to heal and he must find support elsewhere, asking for help. And, even if family members avow they will never trust the addict again, over time, as they see consistent trustworthy behavior, they will likely start extending trust again—even though the family recognizes that reopening trust leaves them vulnerable to being hurt again."

An enabler or co-dependent can't control the addict or his addiction; therefore, he must decide not to be controlled by the person or her disease. It is possible to detach himself from the unhealthy relationship, relearning to focus on his own life rather than on the life of the addict.

With love, the enabler must say, "I did not cause your addiction and I cannot cure it. I now recognize I cannot stop your addiction, and I acknowledge I do not own the right or responsibility to manage it or you. Still, I have let it shape and even control my life. Your addiction has grown to be my addiction, and I will no longer accept or permit that. The only person who can help you is yourself. You are responsible for your own behavior." Separating from the adverse impact another person's addiction has on the enabler or co-dependent's life not only frees the "helper" but also forces the addict to deal with his own issues.

Such a detachment does not mean deserting the addict—it is not unkind. The detaching should be in love, occurring without judgment or condemnation of the person—it does not require abandoning the addict or withholding love. It does require an end to rescuing the person from his own actions and their consequences. The enabler must stop surrendering to the demands and needs of the addict. Though difficult, the enabler must decide not to let the crises of the addict's life control his own life. While it is heartbreaking to allow a loved one to destroy her life, the enabler must acknowledge his own actions can't save the addict. By helping the addict, he is prolonging the addiction. Admitting that previous attempts at rescuing the addict have not ended the addiction is the first step toward moving from enabling or co-dependency to tough love.

When family members detach and the addict is faced with the reality of his situation, he discerns the "game is ending"—that denial and manipulation will no longer push the enabler or co-dependent into a support and rescue role. Then, or later, the addict has to assume responsibility for his own life. And when he does, we should be there for him. Detaching does not mean we should not be supportive if/when the addict decides to get help.

CHAPTER 9

THE BAIT STORES

(The availibility of drugs)

$\mathfrak{M}$ichael Mooney began a March 2010 article about the pipeline of pain pills this way: "Florida has given the rest of America so much over the years: delicious orange juice, great football players, cop dramas, a preposterous quantity of Disney paraphernalia, and more recently, the devastating social destruction of prescription pill addition." The latter is a gift that just keeps on giving.

A Broward County Grand Jury report on the proliferation of drug clinics in South Florida summarized the root of the problem: "Beginning in 2002, and continuing for the next seven years, the Florida Legislature failed, in spite of repeated bills brought before it, to enact legislation to implement a Prescription Drug Monitoring Program (PDMP). PDMPs provide an electronic database from which doctors, pharmacists and law enforcement officers can track the dispensation of prescription drugs to patients. In early 2009, thirty-eight (38) states had enacted legislation implementing such programs. Thirty-two (32) of the states' PDMPs were in effect, while six were waiting to go online." The largest state without a PDMP, Florida became a lucrative pipeline for traffickers, dealers, and users seeking to illegally acquire prescription drugs.

Until it finally passed a law in the fall of 2010 to try to curb the easy access, Florida was not only the largest of the dozen or so states without a monitoring system, it also claimed 92 of the nation's top 100 dispensers of oxycodone, according to the Drug Enforcement Administration. Even with the law, slowing down the outflow of drugs will not come soon. The law is being challenged in federal court, and it is questionable if it will ever be funded adequately even if it withstands the constitutional challenges it faces.

THE I-75 DRUG CORRIDOR

Wayne Bird, chief of police in the southernmost Kentucky town on I-75, told Mooney that pain pills make up 85 to 90 percent of all arrests made by his officers—accounting for seven of ten traffic stops. He asserts that the vast majority of the pills he confiscates come from pain clinics in Broward and Palm Beach counties. Worse than that, most of the people in the town's jail in 2010 were there "'because of something they did while on pills, something they did to get pills, or because they were caught possessing pills illegally.'" Mooney notes that Florida law enforcement officers have nicknamed these Kentucky mountain people "Pillbillies."

According to the Broward County Grand Jury report, without a Prescription Drug Monitoring Program being enforced, "Drug traffickers, dealers and users easily engage in illegal doctor shopping to acquire prescription drugs. They travel to multiple doctors several times a day, week, or month in search of physicians who willingly prescribe and supply them prescription drugs. If ethical and conscientious doctors refuse to sell them drugs, they travel from pain clinic to pain clinic attempting to find an unscrupulous physician willing to supply them drugs."

The Bait and Tackle Shops

Patients seeking drugs go to clinics or other medical facilities and engage in the "two-step dance" with the doctor. Typically, they fake illnesses and complain of pain they don't have. Sometimes they come with altered MRI's in hand. Sometimes the MRIs don't show any injuries, but a statement by the patient that he is in pain, combined with a cursory exam lasting three or four minutes, is enough to get a 30-day supply of various narcotics, a mixture called a cocktail.

The availability of prescription pain pills in South Florida is astounding: In 2009 Broward County had more pain clinics than McDonalds' restaurants. Even more amazing, Mooney reports, "...with a wad of cash and a willingness to hit up several of these pill mills, someone could easily procure 1,000 pills in a single afternoon." Buying the pills at $5 each and selling them illegally in Kentucky and neighboring states for $80 to $100 each makes a nice profit. Or, as Mooney describes it, "a very profitable smuggler's run."

Destination: Kentucky

Chief Bird says until a few years ago he had never found a syringe in a drug stop, even with cocaine. But now, syringes are everywhere. Addicts know the quickest way to get oxycodone into their blood streams is to melt the pills on a spoon or piece of foil and suck the resulting liquid into a syringe for injecting straight into a vein.

Why Kentucky? Although illegal sales of prescription drugs are on the rise across the United States, Bird thinks the extreme poverty of his area is a factor for the Florida-Kentucky pipeline. Drugs make people feel better about living in poverty—or at least numbs them so they don't care. Alternatively, some of the pill buyers/sellers aren't hooked themselves; they just found the only high-paying job available to them.

Broward County and Palm Beach Counties

According to the previously mentioned Grand Jury Report, "The number of pain clinics has skyrocketed in South Florida. From August 2008 to November 2009, a new pain clinic opened in Broward and Palm Beach counties on average every three days."

The report reveals an increase from four pain clinics in South Florida (all in Broward County) in 2007 to 66 in South Florida (including Broward, Palm Beach and neighboring counties) in 2008. The number continues to swell. As of April 2010, *Time* magazine reported that in South Florida in late 2009, 176 pill mills were operating, an increase of more than 100 new clinics in a 14-month period. Broward hosted 115 of the 176 clinics.

The number of narcotics being administered is mind-boggling. In South Florida, during the last six months of 2008, pain clinics dispensed almost 9 million dose units of oxycodone on site. More than six million of those doses were in Broward County alone. The Broward County Grand Jury report describes the facilities dispensing these outrageous numbers as "rogue clinics putting pills out for cash." Caravans from Kentucky, Michigan, Colorado, and Ohio—and untold other states—bring throngs of people to South Florida to seek their drug of choice, usually the pain killer Oxycontin (oxycodone) and the anti-anxiety medicine Xanax. The tackle box is full of lures, and they wiggle with soft colors and careless charm in front of addicts craving relief. All it takes to bite the hook is a couple of lies and a handful of cash.

Hillsborough County

On the other side of the state from Broward County, Tampa has its own bevy of pain clinics. An undercover detective with the Hillsborough County Sheriff's Office called it "the land of zombies." Florida's lax monitoring of prescription drugs draws in both doctors who open pain clinics and addicts who like the easy supply of drugs.

An article in the *St. Petersburg Times* described one couple from Mississippi who had appointments with 12 different doctors in Florida on the day they were arrested in May 2010. They admitted they paid about $1 per pill in pharmacies in Hillsborough County and sold them for up to $30 each when they returned to Mississippi. Some of the clinics see more than 200 patients a day, charging $250 for initial visits and $100 for return patients. One 14-month criminal investigation in Hillsborough County ending in March 2010 discovered a pain clinic operating with five physicians had administered more than 2 million of the highly addictive oxycodone pills in one year, according to federal court documents. It's more than an epidemic—it's a pandemic. And the deaths from overdose surge as the drug plague increases.

Attempts to Slow Down the Pipeline

If the pain clinics have their day in court, their numbers won't be diminishing any time soon. They are fighting the law passed by the Florida legislature that prohibits felons from owning pain clinics, sets stricter criteria for doctors who prescribe and dispense pain medication, and restricts advertising by pain clinics, as well as restricting sale of drugs for cash. (Until the new law passed, a person operating a pain clinic in Florida didn't even have to be a medical doctor, and billboards along the highway advertised the pain clinics.) Attorneys representing several pain clinics in the state, two other doctors, and a patient joined in filing a federal lawsuit in October 2010, challenging the law as unconstitutional.

In the meantime, in Florida alone, deaths related to prescription drug use rose from 2,780 in 2006 to 3,750 in 2008. That averages about 10 deaths a day—more than the number of fatalities from street drugs like cocaine and heroin. These numbers don't begin to tell the story, since the majority of the drugs travel out of state, where the deaths are not traceable to Florida. All of the deaths have faces. And families who are left devastated by the senseless deaths. One Kentucky parent who lost his beautiful daughter to a drug overdose offered a grim reminder, "The drugs, they don't discriminate and it can happen to anybody."

With Florida moving to tighten its grip on pill mills, operators are moving north into Georgia, which is one of only seven states that still do not have a prescription monitoring program. A March 8, 2011, *Chattanooga Times-Free Press* article reported that cases are on the rise in North Georgia, where doctors who aren't licensed pain management physicians work at special clinics, often writing hundreds of prescriptions for medications such as Oxycontin and Xanax. Catoosa

County, Ga., Sheriff Phil Summers declares that the county's number one drug problem is illegal prescription drug medication—it's become a black plague. Like Florida, these pill mills attract people from long distances and require cash purchases. The article cited a raid in March 2011 that resulted in the arrest of one doctor and the closing of a clinic. Similarly, officials in Calhoun, Ga., shut down a pain clinic less than two weeks later, seizing almost 200,000 pills. Less than three weeks later, both North Georgia clinics had reopened, and the law enforcement officers were forced to return the pills they had confiscated. Making a charge stick is difficult, officials complain. Rick Allen, director of the Georgia Drugs and Narcotics Agency, notes it takes months or years to shut a pill clinic down.

State Representative Tom Weldon (R-Ringgold, Ga.) calls Georgia an "island state" and is drafting a bill to put a prescription monitoring program in place. Whether the bill will pass is questionable. Those opposing the bill express concern about how easily law enforcement could view a patient's history with the proposed database. In the meantime, officials are monitoring the 40 known pill mills in the state, while the number of people who die from prescription overdoses in Georgia has been running six times the number who die of overdose of illegal drugs.

More numbers, more places, and more cases could be cited, but it would be redundant. Suffice it to say, as reported by the National Drug Intelligence Center, "Virtually every interstate and highway in the United States is used by traffickers to transport illicit drugs to and from distribution centers and market areas throughout the country, and every highway intersection provides alternative routes to drug markets." Clearly, the problem is of epic proportions in both distribution and consumption. The route beginning in Florida is just one example, albeit one of the worst of the eight principal corridors through which most illicit drugs and drug proceeds are transported to and from market areas.

FROM THE CLINICS TO DEALERS TO THE ADDICT
Back closer to home, the addict craving a fix only has to find someone who has a Florida source or some other pill chain. For Sylvia, it was a lady in a nearby town who ran the bait store. Her supply came from prescription drugs addicts sold to buy street drugs. Generally, her sources went to multiple doctors in Chattanooga and surrounding cities, where they obtained prescriptions, had them filled, and then traded with the bait store dealer. *By the time the dealer handed the pills to me, they were sometimes dirty and smelled of cigarette smoke, but I didn't care—I took them anyway because the craving was stronger than my repulsion. But I*

sometimes wondered how many germs were on the pills as I swallowed them. The lady's own daughter dead from an overdose, she bought and sold drugs to support her two grandchildren. She never touched a pill herself, and she even warned Sylvia she was taking too many—but she never refused to sell them to her.

The drugs and alcohol are available if you want them; you just have to choose not to bite the bait.

PART THREE

CHAPTER 10

UNHOOKED AND HOPEFUL:

Terry C's Personal Story

$t$he whimsical art lining the foundation of the building where Terry's art studio is housed gives a colorful clue about the man inside. Old pieces of ceramic—birds, cups, sharks, flowers, plates, bottles, and myriad other objects—form a lively, multi-hued welcome to the place where Terry has become the man he was destined to be. The road he traveled to get there was rocky, sometimes treacherous. At times, he came close to falling from the cliff of addiction where he teetered on the abyss of his wretched life.

The oldest of three children, Terry knew something was not quite right at an early age. "I didn't feel comfortable in my own skin." Sociable and out-going, his mom and dad didn't know how to deal with their eldest, who preferred a drawing tablet to playing with other kids. School was troublesome—from the second grade where Terry began skipping school until he was kicked out of two high schools. It wasn't that he was drinking all that much; he was just being mischievous.

Terry's errant ways caught up with him when he was 20. Marginally involved with guys who robbed a convenience store, Terry went along for the ride, equipped with a whiffle ball bat. But his weapon of choice didn't make a difference to the judge—he was sentenced to jail for armed robbery, along with his gun-toting pals. "I felt bad about myself," he remembers, but his shame wasn't strong enough to force him to change.

When he was released from prison several months later, Terry got a job in a restaurant/bar and not only went back to drinking but also started smoking pot. The high he felt from marijuana not only rejuvenated him—it made him feel good about himself for the first time in years, a sensation worth repeating.

Terry's drinking and drug use escalated for the next few years. All through his twenties, he kept glugging down stronger alcoholic drinks and ingesting heavier and heavier drugs. When he graduated from doing cocaine to crack cocaine, his old friends began to distance themselves, and his family dissociated, having tried everything they knew to save him.

By the age of 28, with no place to live, Terry was moving from couch to couch wherever he could find a "friend" to put him up for a night. If he couldn't locate a welcome mat, he stayed in an empty building. That's where he was one night when, in a blackout, he set out on a rampage and smashed some storefront windows. The police came the next morning, but he didn't even remember where he had been or what he had done the night before. While they searched the apartment where he had been sleeping off his hangover, he slithered out the door and scampered to his grandmother's. "You can wear out everybody else," Terry says with a wry smile, "but not a grandmother."

Knowing the police were after him, Terry bought a bus ticket and headed to Louisiana, where an uncle, who was also drinking and doing drugs, put him up. After three or four weeks in New Orleans, Terry came to the end of his rope: "I just hurt—physically, mentally, and spiritually. I didn't know how to not hurt." Ready to give up on his miserable life, he gulped down a handful of his uncle's prescription pills. Then, having second thoughts, he dialed 911, but when they asked him for his address, he didn't know it. "I just hung up the phone and thought, 'This is how it ends.'"

But it wasn't Terry's time to die. The next morning his uncle woke him, wanting to know where his guns were. "They were missing," Terry recalls, "but I didn't remember taking them." And, although Terry had no recollection of driving the evening before, he had wrecked his uncle's car. The whole night was a blank page, but it clearly wasn't white. It was as dark as midnight in moonless woods.

Knowing Terry had likely taken the guns to kill himself, Terry's uncle didn't want any part of that. "You're going to die," he admonished Terry, "but I'm not going to let you depart this life in my house."

Back in Chattanooga, alone with no one he felt he could call for help, Terry took the last money he had to get a room at the Holiday Inn and bought a quart of cheap whiskey, knowing he would have to be drunk to follow through with his intent to kill himself. "I decided hanging would be my only choice since I didn't have enough pills and didn't own a gun. While I was trying to figure out how I could do it without pain, a clear thought suddenly penetrated my murky brain: 'Life's not supposed to be over at 28.'"

Lucid for the first time in months, Terry called his younger brother. Soon, his father and brother came to pick him up. Terry was in sad shape, and his father stayed up with him all night. They talked and talked, his father asking questions about his life over the past few years. For the first time, Terry opened up and told the truth about his despicable life and the terrible things he had done and experienced—ranging from stealing from his family to getting stabbed so badly he almost died.

The next morning, Terry's mother confronted him: "Do you want help?"

"I guess I need it, Mom," Terry responded.

"Then you need to go find it."

The parents intuitively knew Terry must take responsibility for his own healing. He didn't have insurance and certainly didn't have any money. He didn't even have a driver's license.

Desperate, Terry called CADAS (Council for Alcohol and Drug Abuse Services) and was told the treatment facility would admit him, but it would be a week before they had an open bed. "I sat paralyzed in my parents' house that week. I couldn't go outside; I knew I had warrants on my head." Laughingly, Terry divulges it was probably good he didn't know he could enter CADAS with drugs or alcohol in his system, so he quit cold turkey. He had temporarily let go of the bait, but he wasn't unhooked.

Looking back, Terry admits that, although he knew he needed help, he went to CADAS for the wrong reason—to escape being arrested. During his 28 days in in-patient treatment, though, he acknowledges, "Something began to happen to me. I saw other people getting hope and thought, 'If this is working for them, it might work for me.'" But a major obstacle confronted Terry: "They kept talking about God, about turning the care of your life over to Him." Terry didn't like the sound of that: "If I do that, I'm not going to have any fun." And fun was what life was all about.

Then, one night as Terry looked across the room and saw his old suitcase, an epiphany hit like a floodlight flipping on, "All I have is a suitcase with a few clothes. I don't have much to give up, so what am I worrying about?" In an experience Terry describes as "almost like an altar call," he told God, "Take this suitcase, this wreck of a life. I'm not doing too well with it. I'm ready to let you take control." With that forlorn plea, a long-awaited sense of peace flooded Terry like a gentle spring rain, cleansing him. "Things changed that night on the outside and on the inside. I started doing what people told me to do to get well."

At the end of his 28-day treatment, Terry entered a half-way house that took indigents. There, he found help in getting a factory job (a place he concedes he would never have worked before his life crashed). With no car and no false pride, he walked from the half-way house to the factory. And he worked on continuing the Twelve Steps. His counselor recommended attending three AA meetings a week. Terry went to one every day and sometimes added a second one. He was committed to staying unhooked and hopeful.

As he worked on recovery, Terry felt a divine hand in his life. "Because I was doing what I was supposed to do, miracles began to happen." A week before he had to leave the half-way house (after having begged an additional two months beyond the maximum of three normally allowed), a small apartment opened up across the street. With his new income, Terry could afford it.

Thankful for his newfound life of sobriety, Terry wanted to give back, so he began volunteering at CADAS. After six months, another miracle—he was offered a fulltime job, working with other addicts. Looking back, Terry thinks being involved with CADAS, and later other treatment centers, during his first years of sobriety gave him strength and courage to stay clean. As a counselor, he knew what it was like to be down and out, so he didn't beat up on recovering addicts. He helped them see where they had been and encouraged them to decide where they were going.

Often, Terry asked his patients, "What has your addiction robbed you of?" He reminded them everyone has a gift, and he challenged each patient to follow his dream. "Own it," he encouraged, "don't be afraid of what will happen when you commit to use your gift."

After giving this speech a couple thousand times, Terry concedes he faced his own reality: "I wasn't using my talent." He started making art, at first just for himself, and he hasn't stopped since. He learned he didn't have to be perfect—he just had to please himself. And, when he started doing that, people began to tell him he was good, so good that he should get his work in art galleries. Although he was still working in the treatment field, he managed to create art whenever he wasn't working and began showing his colorful, capricious collages.

About this time, Terry met Deanna, who would later become his wife. A physician who had just finished her residency, she encouraged Terry's commitment to his talent, often traveling to art shows with him. Slowly, his art began to take more and more of his time, and he finally made a fulltime commitment to his creative work.

Today, friends say, "You can't get from where you were to where you are today." (Where he is today is a happily married father of two young boys and an artist whose work is so good he not only is successful financially but also has given back to his community by helping restore an old part of his hometown.) Terry responds to his friends: "I didn't get from where I was to where I am today. God did it."

As for the outstanding warrants, after his first six months of sobriety, Terry turned himself in with the help of an attorney who was in recovery himself. After listening to Terry's story, he told Terry, "I'm going to help you," though Terry was upfront about not having any cash. In court, with his father standing beside him, Terry told the judge about his recovery. Seeing sincerity in Terry's eyes, the compassionate judge sentenced him to "one year of doing what you are doing—staying sober, going to AA."

As Terry walked out with his attorney, he turned to him and asked, "How much do I owe you?" Tears threatening his eyelids, Terry shares the attorney's response: "I'm not going to charge you anything. You've got the rest of your life to make amends—you'll pay it back."

And Terry has done just that, although he found that going up to someone and saying, "I wronged you," isn't easy. "But it has to be done," he says, "if you are going to live with yourself."

Recollecting he was the guy who would do anything, Terry tells about a time a friend asked him to steal a blue bike from a man's front porch because the man owed his friend money. A daredevil who liked a challenge, Terry didn't hesitate. Years later, with a flinch, Terry saw the man at an AA meeting. His conscience fully charged, he thought, "I'm going to have to tell him." But, his courage faltering, Terry also reasoned, "Maybe he won't stay sober and won't come back to the meetings." But the man did, and then one day he showed up to play golf at a course where Terry played. The little man inside Terry's head didn't give him any slack this time: "You're going to have to tell him, Terry." Unable to escape, Terry walked up to the man and confessed he had stolen the man's bike from his front porch many years ago.

"My blue bike?" the man questioned, starting to cry. "I had a DUI, and that bike was my only transportation." Terry felt so bad he almost wept himself. He offered to pay the man for the bike, but the man said it wasn't necessary. Finally, after he discovered the man needed new golf clubs, Terry bought him a set.

The man would never have known Terry was the thief who made off with his bike, but Terry knew. "Part of being sober is making things right," he avows, "even if the other person doesn't know."

Making amends became a way of life for Terry, even though he sometimes cringed before making the plunge. Forgiving himself came easier. "When I grasped the fact that I was an alcoholic, that was huge," he says. "For years, I thought I was crazy; when I realized I was sick, it wasn't a big issue to forgive myself for the bad things I had done."

Recognizing his addiction was a disease freed him from guilt, but Terry asserts it was God who healed him, who helped him release the power of his creativity. Today, his studio abounds with capricious artwork carefully crafted from castoffs. Each work of art has stories of the lives whose once treasured possessions became junk to someone and then found new life in Terry's artwork. As we looked around the gallery, we wondered how much of Terry's life is in the broken pieces.

Sitting with us, talking freely and openly about his past, Terry is finally comfortable in his own skin. Looking at him, one would never know he was once hooked and entangled in the underbrush of addiction. Unhooked and hopeful, auburn hair framing his face in soft ringlets, Terry's ruddy complexion glows with peace and contentment. Occasionally, his expression slips into sadness as he recalls his youthful follies, but he quickly regains his effervescent outlook, cheerful about his work and his future. His jeans could be a painting of his life—colorful splotches of paint forming irregular shapes, creating a unique being whose blemishes add character to his strikingly handsome appearance. Undoubtedly, one of the ceramic plaques affixed to his studio's exterior foundation speaks a truism Terry lives: "To have enough to share—to know the joy of giving; To thrill with all the sweets of life is living."

CHAPTER 11

CHOICES

Until a person can say deeply and honestly, "I am what I am today because of the choices I made yesterday," that person cannot say, "I choose otherwise."

STEPHEN R. COVEY

We are all imperfect human beings living in an imperfect world. Haloes tilted and scratched, we feel "bedraggled, beat-up, and burnt-out." Brennan Manning, a recovering alcoholic who penned these descriptive words, knows from experience that addicts are "earthen vessels who shuffle along on feet of clay." He wrote *The Ragamuffin Gospel* for people like himself—"for the wobbly and weak-kneed who know they don't have it altogether and are too proud to accept the handout of amazing grace." Those who are "bent and bruised," he says, "feel that their lives are a grave disappointment to God," and their guilt is compounded because they also feel they have failed themselves, their families, and their friends.

Weary and discouraged from feeling powerless over their dependence on drugs or alcohol, addicts wonder if their lives will always be full of frustration, failure, and regret. Is there a way out of the abyss of addiction into which so many have fallen?

Monteleone maintains, "Addicts have a pattern of reacting to stressors of life that is destructive. Most often, this is not caused by a personality disorder. Instead, it's just the way addicts have learned to manage their lives, resulting from a compulsive manifestation of feelings. Emotions prompt behavior, and addicts must learn that the hot buttons triggering their destructive behaviors are inside themselves, not outside."

Monteleone emphatically declares, "Other people can't push your button—only you can do that. If an addict believes other people can push his buttons, he has handed over the power to control himself. He must develop the mindset and skills to take back the power for his behavior.

"To move from being a victim to accepting responsibility," Monteleone knows, "the person must look for options, ask clarifying questions, and negotiate supportive outcomes." In essence, the addict must choose how she acts on her feelings.

An addict fears what it will be like to live without drugs or alcohol, asking, "Can I face my problems without numbing my mind?" Only when the pain of living with drugs exceeds the fear of living without them is the addict at a place where she admits her need and seeks help. Only then will she choose to stop her dependence on substances that alter her feelings but don't solve her problems.

The wake-up call may be a job loss, an arrest, an overdose, or just a slow realization that substance abuse doesn't make life better—it makes it intolerably worse.

Facing who she is and what she is takes courage—and it is a choice only the addict can make. She can choose to hide from her problems, drowning them in alcohol or masking them with drugs; or, she can choose to tackle them. And, if she makes no choice at all, that is in itself a choice.

CHOICE 1
Stop Lying — Admit Your Addiction
Admitting he is an addict—that he is powerless over his addiction and that his life is unmanageable—is the addict's first step toward freedom. Denial demands emotional energy. Truth frees up this reservoir of power to be used in positive ways and sets him free from all of the terrible lies he tells himself and others.

It isn't easy to let go of what the addict has been hiding inside; looking at the mess he has made of his life is painful. Seeing the damage he has done, some of it irreparable, is like looking at a painted canvas ripped by a reckless scalpel. But it is what it is. It is what the addict became and what he did when he allowed himself to be influenced by substance abuse. As Covey notes in the quote above, the addict must acknowledge that he is what he is today because of the choices he made in the past. Then, and only then, can he make different choices for his future.

Admitting addiction helps close the door on what the addict was and opens the door to what he can become. Shame and regret will not change the past. As Shakespeare wrote, "What's gone and what's past help should be past grief." Dwelling on past problems and injuries wastes emotional energy that can be diverted to a new life.

The addict will also find, as R. D. Laing noted, "The truth brings with it a great measure of absolution, always." Facing the past with honesty brings freedom and release—necessary for tackling a future without succumbing to the lure of lethal bait.

CHOICE 2
Seek Help

If the addict is powerless over her addiction, how can she have hope?

Addiction is a disease that attacks on three fronts: physical, mental, and spiritual. To recover from the disease, all three aspects must be treated.

Narcotics Anonymous describes physical addiction as "the compulsive use of drugs: the inability to stop using once we have started." The body's chemistry has been infiltrated, and if the ingestion of drugs or alcohol is halted, withdrawal symptoms can be dramatic and dreadful. Sudden withdrawal can even result in death. To ensure safe withdrawal, an addict needs to have medical intervention. Medical assistance won't eliminate the horrors of detoxification, but it can monitor vital systems of the body and minimize effects.

The mental aspect of the disease, according to NA, "is the obsession, or overpowering desire to use, even when we are destroying our lives." The person becomes dependent not just physically, but also emotionally, on drugs or alcohol to get through life's daily ups and downs. Concealing the reality of problems that may have initiated the abuse and complicated rather than resolved them, the addict uses drugs or alcohol as a crutch to help her walk through each day. Hang-ups and hurts are hidden, but they do not cease to exist. To deal with the core issue underlying addiction, counseling and other support systems are necessary. Fortunately, most treatment centers address not only physical but also mental/emotional symptoms of addiction, identifying root problems and helping the addict learn appropriate coping mechanisms.

The third aspect of addiction, spirituality, encompasses the individual's self-centeredness—the feeling that "I" can do this alone: "I can stop whenever I want to—I don't need anyone to help me." Only when the addict accepts that she must turn her addiction—and her life—over to a power greater than herself can she find relief from the intolerable pain of addiction. NA is careful not to prescribe the higher power: "We made a decision to turn our will and our lives over to the care of God as we understand Him."

This spiritual transformation takes an addict from the destructive place where her total being—body, mind, and spirit—was dominated by drugs or alcohol to a place where control is handed over to the higher power. Powerless herself, she gives the reigns to an all-powerful being who can take the broken pieces of her life and glue them back into a beautiful vessel. Not perfect, but glorious in all its imperfections. The mended cracks in the vessel don't make it less strong or less striking. They are reminders of the past, and at the same time, markers for a future where "fears are lessened, and faith begins to grow as we learn the true meaning of self-surrender," as described in NA. Inside the safety of the repaired spirit, she no longer has to fight fear, anger, guilt, self-pity, or depression. NA continues by averring that the Power who brought the addict to the program stays with the person and will continue to guide her if she will allow it. With that promise, the paralyzing fear of failure and hopelessness slowly falls away and is replaced with assurance that, with the help of her higher power, the addict can live free of drugs and alcohol. Unhooked and hopeful.

CHOICE 3
Accept the Past and Move On

Earlier we talked about guilt and shame both causing and resulting in addicts' destructive behaviors. Under the influence of drugs or alcohol, culpability is often repressed or at least softened by the substance of choice. When an addict becomes sober, he must find a way to live with his conscience. Recovery does not mean he can wave a magic wand and his past will disappear; the consequences of his actions must still be faced. Even so, they no longer have to be a violent wind endlessly thrashing the addict's future.

Regrets that attack the addict as he begins his new life of sobriety will pull him down unless he chooses to use them in a different way—to give him perspective for how he wants his future NOT to be played out. Repeating "if only," looking backward too often and too long, can prevent the addict from living in the present and planning for the future. "Some people focus on the past to the extent," Baker says, "that their rearview mirror gets bigger than their windshield. With this kind of driving, forward progress is nearly impossible. In fact," he adds, "a crash is likely in the near future."

Spiritual growth helps the recovering addict keep his eyes looking forward rather than backward. When he brings his past to his higher power, he can let go and let God deal with it.

Unfortunately, many people don't let go easily even when they try. They can tie their past actions, guilt, and shame into a huge garbage bag and toss it as far as they can into the ocean. "There," they say. "I'm through thinking about my past problems and sins." But a short time later, if God hasn't solved their problems quickly enough, they find they have left a long piece of twine attached to the garbage bag, and they tug it back to shore, retaking the responsibility for worrying. This happens repeatedly until they are willing to cut the cord and let the garbage of their lives be enveloped by the ocean of their higher power.

CHOICE 4

Adjust Your Perspective

Returning to life after addiction gives a person the freedom to reignite her belief system. What she learned and forgot will come back to her—she will once again see what is really important in life. Changing her focus from her own problems and hurts to others' needs will give her new purpose. Loren Eiseley's well-known starfish story vividly illustrates this point:

Walking on a deserted stretch of beach one day, a young man questioned the impact of the self-appointed task of an old man who was tossing starfish back into the water.

"Old man," he challenged, "why are you wasting your time? There are miles and miles of beaches with starfish—you can't possibly make a difference."

The old man glanced sideways, acknowledging the words, then picked up yet another starfish and slung it into the ocean before responding, "Made a difference to that one." The young man went on his way, but he was troubled, and the next morning, he walked to a spot near the older man, reached down, and skipped a starfish across the water toward restored life.

Both men, one sooner than the other, realized true joy comes from giving of one's self, making a difference one starfish at a time—a starfish who will die without help. Addiction is a self-centered disease, forcing a person to be a "taker" rather than a "giver." True peace and happiness comes from within—not from other people or possessions. When an addict changes her perspective, she can find courage to persist toward recovery even when facing overwhelming odds.

At some point in the miracle of his sobriety, Terry decided, "There was a time I didn't have a choice in taking the next drink. It was different in recovery. I knew, 'If I drink again, now it's on me.'" In other words, when he was addicted, the chemicals in his brain controlled his "gotta have it" cravings. Once he was unhooked, he could no longer use a rewired brain circuit as the rationale for making a bad choice. In control of his mind, he would be responsible. The perspective of an addict can always conjure up an excuse; the perspective of a recovering addict leaves no room for false justification.

CHOICE 5
Love Yourself

All love, it seems, is conditional. Our parents love us if we sit still in church, make good grades, or stay out of trouble. Our friends love us if we listen to their dreams and complaints, supporting and nurturing them. Our subordinates at work love us if we give them raises and praise their work. But if we fail to meet all expectations of everyone who loves us, however unrealistic they may be, we slide off our pedestal. As the old saying goes, "You can please some of the people all of the time and all of the people some of the time, but you can't please all of the people all of the time." Unless we submit to everyone's whims and wants, it seems, we aren't worthy of love.

Life has taught us that limitations and weaknesses diminish our image; and under the control of alcohol or drugs, an addict soon finds he can't do enough good to make up for all the bad he does. Even if others don't condemn him, he disparages himself as he may have as a child—if he wrecked his mother's new car, the guilt he felt was far greater than the anger spewing from her lips. And that doesn't compare to the thrashing he gives himself when he tries without success to justify damaged relationships and destroyed lives.

Even when an addict makes the first step toward sobriety, past mistakes haunt him. Knowing he has broken his world, he berates himself for his lack of willpower and actions that brought pain to others. They may or may not be ready to forgive him, but it matters not. The greatest accuser of an addict always remains the addict himself.

Recovery will be much easier if the recovering addict lets up on himself—allowing a break from self-recrimination. Seeking words to describe the inner anguish of knowing he has violated his integrity and has hurt people he cares for is not helpful. The addict should accept that he is worthy of love despite his past actions, recognizing bad behaviors didn't make him a bad person—he had a disease that distorted his thinking. He must believe in himself and the person he was before drugs and alcohol and the person he will be after they are abandoned. In short, when he becomes unhooked, the addict must learn to love himself again.

Terry's charity toward himself eventually helped him to return to the love of his life—art. As a kid, all of his free time was spent drawing. In his 20s, he channeled that same energy into drinking and drug use. "I excelled at that," he admits. When he heard Charlie Lukas, a famous folk artist from Alabama, tell kids, "If you can unscrew a whiskey bottle, you can unscrew a paint jar," he realized that a person can also unscrew a different bottle and pour his emotions into that. That insight allowed him to redirect his energies to his inner being, where not only his spirit lay impoverished, but his art talent had lain dormant. As Pablo Picasso once said, "Every child is an artist. The problem is how to remain an artist once he grows up." When Terry could love himself again, he could once more love his creative spirit. He could be an artist again.

CHOICE 6

Be Hopeful

Denis Waitley tells of a dark night during World War II when sirens blared and lights went out during an air raid drill as he sat with his grandmother at their home in San Diego. Nine years old, he fearfully asked his grandmother, "Will the Japanese beat us in the war and take us over?"

Denis' grandmother shushed him, reassuring him it would never happen. "They will bring upon themselves what they have put in. They have, by their own actions, sown the seeds of their own destruction." To support her contention, she went to her room and came back with a handwritten copy of a speech she had seen in a newspaper. The speech had been broadcast on the radio by the First Lady of China, Madame Chiang Kai-shek, who led her people in their stalwart fight against the Japanese. Although she had not copied the speech word-for-word, Denis' grandmother read what she had written:

"If the past has taught us anything it is that every cause brings its effect, every action has a consequence. We Chinese have a saying: 'If a man plants melons, he will reap melons; if he sows beans, he will reap beans.' And this is true of everyone's life; good begets good, and evil leads to evil....In the end, we are all the sum total of our actions....Thus also, day by day, we write our own destiny; for inexorably...we become what we do."

It is never too late to plant a garden of hope. If the addict chooses to sow seeds of self-transformation, she will reap a life of joy, peace, and happiness. Just as seeds do not shake the dirt from around their heads overnight, neither will the recovering addict emerge from the rotten soil of her life quickly. And, just as the plants take weeks and months to develop, so will her new life grow.

The gardener can help plants grow strong and straight if she tends them—pulling weeds when they sprout, long before they are large enough to overwhelm budding flowers or vegetables. In transforming her life, the addict must likewise keep destructive habits or people from crowding out her positive growth. In addition, just as plants need water and fertilizer, feeding the spirit with study and prayer nourishes her inner being and makes her strong on the outside.

As Galations 6:7 predicts and as Madame Chiang knew, "Whatsoever a man soweth, that shall he also reap." This is true for the saint and the sinner alike, so undoubtedly the addict will reap what she sows. If she plants seeds of hopefulness and nurtures them, the garden of her life will flourish. She will find fresh starts, new dreams, and restored belief in herself and others.

CHAPTER 12

UNHOOKED AND HOPEFUL:

Nicole H's Personal Story

On the outside, Nicole looks like a fashion model—and indeed, she has done some modeling—but on the inside, she feels ugly. If you met her on the street, you'd admire her long, light blondish-auburn hair, her curvy body, and her chic clothes. But when you talk to her, you quickly realize she has had a darker side; she has been places and done things with her body that now haunt her.

From the beginning, Nicole's life wasn't ideal. In fact, something in her early years was so traumatic she repressed all memory of her childhood before the age of 10. She does know her father was addicted to alcohol and drugs and that he had affairs, causing her parent to separate. (All of the siblings of Nicole's father also had addiction problems, some with alcohol and some with prescription drugs. Undoubtedly, Nicole inherited DNA that predisposed her to addiction.)

Her parents' issues took a toll on Nicole, and she started drinking when she was 14. By the age of 16, she was imbibing heavily. At 17, she attended a party with some other teenagers because adults promised them alcohol. Before she knew what was happening, a very drunk Nicole was raped by a 36-year-old man. Although the man was arrested after Nicole went through the humiliating experience of a rape kit, a jury deemed Nicole was not a credible witness because she had been intoxicated. The experience left Nicole in pain and frustrated that the justice system let the man get away with raping her. To dull her mental turmoil, she drank more and more and began to add drugs to help her escape the terrible memory. Today, she admits her drug use started in an attempt to numb herself but continued from her love of partying.

For almost a year, Nicole used LSD two or three times weekly. Eventually, the escalating drug use left her extremely depressed, and she was tempted to take her own life. But she kept partying, having a good time. One night, when she was 19, she pulled in the driveway with her boyfriend just shy of her mother's 2 a.m. curfew. As she opened the door to get out of the truck, a man with a mask and gloves, a drink in his hand, approached her. Since it was April Fool's Day, she first thought it was one of her boyfriend's buddies playing a joke. Nicole's boyfriend sat frozen as the man dragged her out of the truck and forced her to get in the back, doing "terrible things" to her. Threatening Nicole's boyfriend with a gun, the man forced him to stay in the truck. Finally unable to stand hearing Nicole's cries, the boyfriend jumped out. The man's attention diverted, Nicole ran to the door of the truck and curled up in a fetal position on the floorboard. Terrified, she heard the gun go off—three times. Fearing the worse, that her boyfriend had been killed, she looked up in surprise as he came around the truck, yelling, "Run, run, run!" Nicole jumped up but fell because her shorts were still around her feet. Her boyfriend pulled her up, and they flew down the driveway, breaking a window to get in the house where her younger sister and mother were sleeping. A call to 911 brought officers, but they questioned her so long the man got away. Once again, the justice system failed Nicole—the man was never caught. They had nothing to go on since the man had worn gloves, leaving no fingerprints.

Today, 16 years later, Nicole still harbors apprehensions, always frightened if she has to be alone. Even installing a security system in her home hasn't helped. Expanding her need to numb emotional pain, Nicole had added fear to the quiver of arrows that relentlessly struck her, sending her deeper and deeper into drugs and alcohol.

At 19, Nicole didn't realize what was driving her; she just knew she needed to get away. When her boyfriend asked her to marry him and move to Atlanta, where he was enrolling at Georgia Tech, she jumped at the chance to run away from her problems. The plan was for her to work while he was going to school, and then she would start college herself. The well-laid plan had to be put on the back burner when she became pregnant two weeks before her husband's graduation. Again, she moved with her husband, this time to Chattanooga, Tn., where he had been offered a good job. Nicole knew her worst fears were about to come true—she was going to be like her mother, dependent on a man for support because she didn't have a good education.

Nicole stopped drinking and taking pills for nine months—until her daughter was born. She also took a few courses at a local community college, but supporting her drug habit (she was back using as soon as the pregnancy ended) and a new child didn't leave enough money for tuition, so she dropped out.

Although she was unhappy and resentful, Nicole wanted to stay off drugs, but multiple trips to the dentist office, resulting from years of neglect when she had no insurance, provided access to prescription pain medicine. By the time the dental work was completed, she was hooked on hydrocodone. Although the dentist eventually cut her off (resulting in a scene that still embarrasses Nicole to talk about), it was too late; her tolerance level had grown and she had to find another source for pain pills, which she says she ate like candy. When she became pregnant again, she managed to stay clean, but coming off hydrocodone and alcohol made her sick and irritable.

Two weeks after the birth of her son, Nicole was back drinking a pint of vodka a day, sometimes more on the weekends. "I pretty much kept a hangover all the time," she admits. "It was all I could do to get out of bed and take care of a baby and a five-year-old. I was kind of 'zombie-ing' through life."

Spiraling out of control, Nicole dropped to 95 pounds, anorexia compounding her abuse. By that point, she couldn't take care of the kids—she couldn't even make it up the stairs of her house, and her mother and husband talked her into going into two rehabilitation programs. She first went to Ridgeview in Atlanta, Ga., for her eating disorder. The experience frightened her: "I thought I was losing my mind, almost like an out-of-the-body experience. I threw up until I had dry heaves. Severely dehydrated, my stomach cramped, and I went from cold sweats to freezing. I couldn't sleep at all while I was coming off alcohol and opiates, but I survived and went from Ridgeview to Valley Hospital in Chattanooga for drug treatment. I was only allowed to stay there seven days, and within a couple of weeks after I was dismissed, I was back on drugs."

Nicole's drug use escalated, and she says, "I lost all self-respect; I was disgusted with myself. I hated the way I looked." Her feelings compounded by postpartum depression, Nicole contemplated suicide. "I was stuck in drug addiction and thought I couldn't get out." Her husband's insurance for drug treatment exhausted, she had nowhere to turn.

For the next three years, Nicole worked as a dancer to support her drug needs. In her words, "I took my clothes off for money." In a dance club environment, drugs were easy to obtain, and Nicole would go from a strip dance where she picked up sixty dollars to one of the drug dealers in the club and back again to earn sixty more dollars, which she promptly handed over to a dealer, time after time, night after night. Her husband knew what she was doing, but he had given up by this time, fed up with Nicole's continuing drug use and uncontrollable behavior.

By now, Nicole says, "I had to get high to get out of bed. I would wake up totally drained." Soon, even the money she made on the dance floor wasn't enough for the pills she needed to get her going and keep her moving. Occasionally, she sold herself for dances outside the club, which meant she was risking arrest for prostitution. One night she thought she would be performing in front of 8-10 men at a private bachelor's party, but 50-60 people showed up. She and another girl had to dance in a four foot square space with guys hovering all over them. "I just kept saying to myself, 'Just do it; get your fix, and get out of here.'" It was good money, but no matter how much she drank or how many pills she took, Nicole hated herself. "I put myself in that situation," she concedes, "and I got to where I had to take downers to sleep and uppers to make it until I could collapse in bed in the early hours of the morning."

"I lost everything," Nicole says somberly. "I lost my self-respect, even my will to live."

Some nights Nicole didn't even make it home. But one morning, she woke up in her bed with a gun on the pillow beside her head. "I didn't even know what I had been doing the night before or how I got home." Her voice shaking, she adds, "What is so scary now is that my kids could have found the gun." After a pause, Nicole says, "I think now of all the situations I put my kids and husband in, and everyone is lucky to be alive."

Another morning Nicole again woke up and didn't remember how she had gotten home. In the driveway, her car sat, parked sideways, with one whole side caved in. In shock that she had driven 25 miles home and didn't even remember, Nicole was also terrified that she might have hit someone when her car sustained the damage now visible in the driveway. Even Oxycontin couldn't contain her fear: "Oh, my God, I may have killed someone," she told her husband.

All day, Nicole sat glued to the internet and television, watching for news of a hit-and-run. Inside she was dying, knowing that "If I find out I killed somebody, I can't live with myself. I will have to kill myself." Over and over she vowed, "If I can get through this, I'm never going to drink and drive again." With a poignant sigh, she adds, "There are not enough stars in the sky to count how many times I have said that."

By nightfall, when no report of a hit-and-run surfaced, Nicole relaxed. She and her husband surmised she must have sideswiped a concrete median barrier. When she realized there were no consequences for her actions, Nicole relaxed. Her husband was so frustrated by the worrisome day, he walked out of the house, saying he had to get away for a while.

As soon as the door closed, Nicole started drinking and taking Oxycontin. The kids were sleeping upstairs, and Nicole had a party on the kitchen floor. She remembers turning off all the lights, lighting a candle, and playing depressing music as she sat there on the floor with a bottle of Jack Daniel's. Crushing some Oxycontin, she began snorting so the drug would hit her more quickly. "I sat there," she says shamefully, "getting messed up again, snorting away, chasing it with the liquor." When she ran out of Oxycontin, she thought, "There is no way I could be out." Desperate, she found some hydrocodone cough syrup (prescribed for her child) in the cabinet, sat down in the floor, and started taking swigs, followed by her chaser of Jack.

"It's amazing I am still alive. I had to have somebody watching over me," Nicole says. "My husband came home and found me passed out on the floor, the candle burned almost out, my hands and arms scarred where I had cut myself with a steak knife." In her stupor, Nicole didn't even remember the self-mutilation. "I'm a glutton for self-pain," she admits.

"I had had a hellacious week," Nicole declares. "The car wreck, the candle incident. . . ."

Today Nicole says she hit bottom when she stopped digging in the nightmarish hole that she had made of her life. Her husband gave her an ultimatum—get help or get out.

"I knew...I knew," Nicole utters softly. "I was sick and tired of being so miserable. At first when I got on drugs they made me feel good. And I tried to tell myself I didn't do drugs or drink in front of my kids. The truth of the matter was I was high around them. I had become a horrible, vicious viper—a shell. I had checked out of myself for a long time." It was time; Nicole agreed, to get help.

Nicole's admission was delayed for about a week to make arrangements for child care. Since she had time on her hands, she decided to have one last fling before she gave up drugs and alcohol for good. She booked a bachelor's party and decided that she would not only dance but do every drug she could find. "I was in major overdrive," she says. "I remember drinking and that there was a lot of cocaine at the warehouse party," which had a stripper pole installed in the second floor living room where the party host lived. Nicole had performed there several times previously since the man not only had lots of money but also "a big mountain of cocaine." Usually, only a couple of guys were there, but this particular night, there were several.

That's about all Nicole remembers of that night. When she arrived home, she was covered in bruises. "There wasn't much skin where I didn't have discolored marks," she acknowledges. As she checked in at Focus Healthcare the next day, she was asked where she got all of the bruises. "I had to look at the admissions counselor and tell him I didn't know—it was so humiliating," Nicole says, adding that she was a blackout drinker and had lots of times when she couldn't remember what happened. When the counselor asked about taking an AIDS test, Nicole hung her head. "Waiting for the results was terrifying. And, if they had been positive (thankfully, they weren't), I couldn't have told them whom I had been with." With sorrow in her eyes, she adds, "That's what it will do to you; you lose self-respect, morals; you lose your entire self."

Nicole was ready for help. She spent 28 days at Focus Healthcare and then a month of intensive outpatient care, followed by weekly aftercare. Today, she still goes daily to AA/NA meetings and keeps regular appointments with her counselor.

With a radiant smile, Nicole says, "Now I wake up each morning and see the sunshine. For years, I lived in such a cloud I didn't care."

Rehab the second time around was a life saver for Nicole. She met a man named Donald who reminded her of her dad, and he became a father figure in her life, just as she became a surrogate daughter for him (his own daughter had died two years previously in a motorcycle accident). Soberly, the man told her, "Invest in a nice dress; you will be attending a lot of funerals." They became good friends, and Nicole even visited with the man and his wife in their home. Sadly, Donald was right—in the year and one half since she was at Focus, she has cried at the burial of four friends she met in treatment. All dead from overdosing after relapse. Tragically, Donald was among the four after having been sober for only six months.

"Without Focus," Nicole says, "I would not have lived." Noting she is definitely of Christian belief, Nicole knows she really grew up with no faith. After everything that happened to her, she began to think there was no God. "If there is a God," she reasoned, "how could he let something like this happen to me?" Still, she believes if she had not had some kind of spirituality left, she would not have survived. "The power of prayer is very much there. I pray; I believe things are going to get better."

Life is better for Nicole; she has had two minor relapses since treatment at Focus, but they only involved alcohol. She reported them and got back on track. On the home front, she and her husband still have issues. He doesn't trust her, and she resents having given up her chance for college when she was younger. She never wanted to be a stay-at-home mom, and she blames her husband for fulfilling his career goals at her expense. Nicole knows she must get rid of her guilt before she can work on her relationship with her husband.

Making amends is tough. Nicole's thankful her spouse has always been there for their children. They remain good friends, and together are trying to make sure their kids grow up in a stable home. For now, they're taking a day at a time, trying to work through their problems so they can stay together.

Nicole is concerned about her little girl, who is now 11-years-old. Ever since Nicole came out of rehab, her daughter won't say, "I love you" to anyone except her cat—not to Nicole, not to her father, not to her brother. Recalling how she herself suppressed the trauma of her childhood, Nicole fears her daughter may be doing the same. She hopes counseling will help.

What Nicole has done to her family fills her with regret—especially for time wasted. But that's behind her, and she is looking to her future.

Nicole plans to enroll in a community college soon, pursuing her dream. With a college degree in hand, maybe she will begin to feel better about herself. She's on the right road, her commitment to recovery motivating her to drive 50 miles round trip daily to meetings where she finds support and encouragement. She's unhooked and hopeful.

CHAPTER 13

RESPONSIBILITY

The willingness to accept responsibility for one's own life is the source from which self-respect springs.

JOAN DIDION

One of the most damaging fallouts of addiction is the loss of self-respect. Whether emanating from self-destructive actions or guilt from hurting people he loves, the addict becomes down on himself, convinced he is a bad person. The way out of the continuous loop of bad behaviors and shame comes only through accepting responsibility for his actions. When he admits his accountability—that he and only he is answerable for his addiction, he takes the first step in rebuilding self-respect. He can be proud of himself for taking charge of his life instead of blaming others for his problems; with this pride comes belief in himself and in his ability to change his life.

THOUGHTS

"Gotta-have-it" thoughts can be partially blamed on serotonin and dopamine levels in the brain, but the addict also faces pressures imposed by society for the "good life" through instant gratification. The reality that she cannot and will not have everything she wants—what she sees others enjoying—is a fact of life. She must stop thinking, "Life is not fair" or "I deserve more" and start considering that possessions don't bring peace and happiness. If that were the case, only poor people would be depressed; only those who couldn't fulfill their life's dreams would be susceptible to addiction.

The addict is responsible for how she thinks and what she thinks when she is not under the influence of alcohol or drugs. Accepting the cards left to play after addictive cards are no longer in the pack, a person learns to live without "have to's" and "gotta have's." One effective strategy for avoiding stepping back into damaging thought patterns is to list the important parts of a person's life. Choosing to think positive thoughts—being thankful for what she has rather than being hung up on life's inequities—helps resist the pull of envy and resentment.

Nell Mohney, inspirational writer, shared the story of one of the world's greatest violists when he broke a string during a concert at Lincoln Center in New York City. Because of polio, Itzhak Perlman walks on crutches, both legs bound by heavy braces. As he moved across the stage with excruciating slowness that night, the audience held its collective breath until he made it to his chair. There, he loosened his braces, placed one foot behind him and extended the other forward before picking up his violin, setting it under his chin, and nodding to the director to begin. After only a few measures, a loud pop sounded over the music. Everyone waited breathlessly to see what the maestro would do. Would he buckle his braces back on and walk painfully off stage to have a new string put on, or perhaps even look for another violin? Mohney says he did neither. After sitting still for a few moments, eyes closed, he signaled the director to continue. Amazingly, he began to play on three strings. Other musicians would have thought it impossible to recompose the music as they played, but Perlman did it masterfully, giving a flawless performance. Mohney notes, "He played the entire piece with power and passion on just three strings." He believed he could do it and he did.

Addicts may have lost one of their strings on the stage of their past life, but they can recompose the present and the future with the three strings they have left. They, like Perlman, just have to believe they can make music with what remains.

DESTRUCTIVE BEHAVIORS

Accepting responsibility for behaviors that have inflicted pain on the addict and his loved ones is critical in rebuilding trust. He may have done unthinkable things—from stealing to emotionally abusing others—and blaming others temporarily covers guilt feelings, but it does not change the facts. Acknowledging his actions, including manipulation of others, opens the door to rebuild relationships.

An addict has two choices—let the destructive behaviors from the past destroy him; or, he can let them refine him just as a silversmith refines silver. The silver must be held in the middle of the fire where the flames are the hottest so the impurities will burn away. Importantly, the silversmith cannot put the silver in the fire and walk away. He must sit in front of the flames the entire time the silver is being refined, never diverting his eyes. For, if the silver stays even a moment too long in the blazing fire, it will be destroyed. How then, one might ask, does the silversmith know when the silver is fully refined? One silversmith had a simple answer, "Oh, that's easy—when I see my image in it."

Destructive behaviors put the addict in a hot fire, but once the impurities have been burned off by accepting responsibility, he can see the image of the person he now is—a recovering addict whose problems have refined rather than destroyed him. In his purified state, he has the strength to restore broken bonds with friends and family.

CONSEQUENCES

Monteleone talks about the difference in how adults and teenagers approach responsibility. She notes, "Adults are responsible for themselves, while teens still have someone to assume responsibility for their actions. Teens are still sorting out boundaries, seeing how much they can get away with. And, they often feel they are superhuman, believing they can survive anything. Adults intellectually understand the possibility of an overdose or an accident while driving under the influence of an addictive substance, but teens think they are indestructible. Consequently, it is more difficult to get them to buy into the concept that addiction is a disease, that it has a hold on them, and that it is not going away. Adults come into treatment with more humility, a more open mind, and more willingness to benefit from the treatment. In contrast, teenagers often have a lot of willfulness.

"Because most teenagers don't truly shift into recovery, relapse isn't the issue—they just continue their abuse because they haven't shifted thinking. Once they are back in their peer group, staying clean isn't usually an option," Monteleone notes.

In the short run, letting others deal with the consequences of addictive behaviors may be appealing. In the long run, it only reinforces the belief that others will always be there to pick up the pieces of the addict's life. Even if they will, does an addict really want someone else taking care of her? Bailing her out of trouble? Controlling how much or how little she will have in life?

Rebuilding self-respect requires the addict to live through the consequences of her actions, not hand them off to other people. Being dependent on others isn't a desirable way of life, and the addict, after a period of time for healing and regrouping, should accept responsibility for what she has made of her life and then work to improve it.

Terry C tells about a man he and his family met while returning from a trip to Florida. "We had stopped at a Starbucks so I could get a couple shots of Expresso," he recalls, "and I noticed the man in line in front of me had two prosthetic legs. But what really caught my attention was the way the guy interacted with his son. He was just 'present.'" As the man ordered four shots of Expresso, he looked at Terry with a smile and said, "My only addiction." With a cragged grin, Terry responded, "Mine, too."

The two men began talking, soon discovering they were both recovering addicts. Exchanging stories, they learned both had been sober for a long time and concurred it was a much better way of life. Terry shared about being forlorn in a lonely hotel room when he took his last drink. The man looked at him with a wry smile. "My last drink, I was laying on a railroad track."

"It takes what it takes," Terry responded. "Some of us take a little more than others, but it's never too late."

PROBLEMS AND HURTS

Life it tough. It isn't fair, and it isn't fun. Children die, marriages fall apart, jobs are lost, health problems occur, catastrophes happen—with or without abuse as a contributing factor. Everyone has disappointments and hurts. But throwing the blame on others for hurts does not help the addict heal. Even if she is not answerable for the hurts, she has to accept the onus for living with them. Taking the stance, "You hurt me, so I'm going to hurt you back" does not take the pain away. Hurts should be written down in sand, where winds of time can erase them. Engraving the hurts in stone keeps them visible, accessible for rehashing and re-wounding.

Mark Twain once remarked that forgiveness is the fragrance the violet leaves on the heel that crushed it. For a violet, that comes naturally. For humans, it comes with an effort, but it can come when the acid of resentment blows away with the sand.

FRIENDS AND PLACES

The recovering addict is accountable for determining where and with whom he spends time. Two of the best strategies for staying sober are to surround himself with people who do not abuse alcohol or drugs and to avoid places where he used the substances that turned his life upside down.

If he drank or used with other people, giving up friends when he gives up substance abuse produces a double loss—two pseudo support systems that must be replaced with a strong and effective system that will encourage his sobriety. NA and AA groups offer such support, as do many church groups, including Celebrate Recovery. And, while not all family members will be there for the addict, most likely will. The key is to seek out and find people who genuinely want to help him stay in recovery. Addicts, as G. Linnaeus Banks wrote in his poem, "What I Live For," should live for those who love them, for those who know them true, for those whose hearts are kind and true. Moreover, as Banks challenged himself, addicts should be in places where they can assist when needed, right wrongs that need righting—for the future, doing whatever good they can do. Living for those one loves and helping those in places of need is a good place to begin responsibility.

COMMITMENT

No one else—regardless of the depth of love or desire—can commit the addict to recovery. Only he can do that. The commitment to get and stay sober must come from deep within—from the realization that the suffering from substance abuse is worse than the pain of facing life sober. Willingness to endure the agony of withdrawal arises from the addict's desire for a better life, pushing him not to flee from problems but to find ways to deal with them. As Terry C puts it, after he reached the jumping off point, where he couldn't imagine living with drugs and couldn't imagine living without them, and had chosen to reach out to something bigger than himself, he didn't want to return to the cliff.

Recovering from addiction is more than just pledging to give up drugs and alcohol; it requires committing to a new way of life—a life that empowers the addict to avoid the destructive thinking and behaviors that brought him to the pit of existence. To stay committed, addicts must learn to take a breather before acting, to be completely honest about feelings, and to reach out for help when down. No one can promise it will be easy, but it is possible to stay unhooked.

An old man who lived in London years ago woke up every morning for 20 years and took a train to the central part of the city, where he sat at a street corner and begged all day. Back at his home, neighbors finally complained because of the stench coming out of his house. Officers who came to investigate were astonished to find small bags of money the man had collected over the years. Counting the money, they realized the beggar was a millionaire. When they shared the good news with him, telling him he no longer needed to beg, the man said nothing. The next morning he woke up, went to the subway, rode the train to his usual street corner, and sat down to beg. Amazingly, this old man had no plan or dream for his life—he just stayed focused on doing what he had always done.

So, too, should addicts stay true to their commitment to recovery. But, they should learn from the beggar. Commitment without a plan takes them nowhere. If the addict doesn't like the conditions of his life in addiction, he must accept responsibility for changing them—not just once but every day for the rest of his life.

What makes people happy is what matters in the end, not what they acquire.

CHAPTER 14

UNHOOKED AND HOPEFUL:

Gary A's Personal Story

$\mathcal{G}$ary A grew up poor, but that wasn't the worst of his problems. His father, a circuit preacher, was a downright drunk. Handsome, charismatic, and eloquent, he charmed his way through life until one day his drinking caught up with him. The next thing Gary knew, his father was out of a job. No one told him what happened, but he later realized his dad had been fired. Perhaps it came to him after one of the many times his dad arrived home so sick he couldn't walk, and one of his friends decided Gary needed to recognize reality: "Your dad isn't sick; he's drunk." It wasn't the first sign and certainly not the last that Gary was growing up in a dysfunctional family; his mom and dad were married and divorced three or four times. His mother wanted him to promise he would never grow up to be like his dad, and Gary swore he wouldn't.

He took his first drink—actually, four beers—on a crisp fall day after a football game in his freshman year of high school. The beers made him aggressive, and soon he was fighting. After that, he swore he would never drink again. He made it a week. By the time he graduated from high school (in the top 10 of his class), he had a drinking problem, accompanied by an attitude problem. The first time he got into a fight after football practice, an assistant coach took him aside and talked to him. They bonded, and it was a connection that brought Gary back to the coach years later when he was desperate for help.

Before that, though, Gary's dad wrecked a school bus (probably while drunk), and as luck would have it, the head coach's son was on the bus. Irate, the coach didn't play Gary in that night's game. Feeling the unfairness of punishment for his dad's sins, Gary quit the team in anger. But the assistant coach was there for him again, telling him, "Quitting is a bad habit to start," and Gary reluctantly returned to the gridiron.

After high school, Gary decided to leave his problems and get out of town, heading to the rugged beauty of the Ozarks as a stunning backdrop for his college days. He lasted all of three days before he got drunk and was kicked out. Humiliated, he came home and enrolled in a local university, but he spent more time drinking than he did going to class and flunked out.

Bored, one Saturday morning, Gary started riding around drinking beer and happened upon a friend. Half-smashed, they decided to hit the sandy shores of Florida for some fun; less than 90 miles later, they realized they were way too drunk to keep driving and crashed at a friend's house in Atlanta. That evening, the friend arranged a date for Gary, who was still feeling the effects of alcohol. He somehow found his way to the girl's home—a huge house towering above him, looking like a mansion to the boy whose early homes had been small and paper thin. Drunk, he chose the largest of three front doors and knocked, but when the door started opening outward, he stepped back and tumbled clumsily into a huge rose bush—unfortunately, one prized by the girl's father. Stuck like a struggling hare in a briar patch, he couldn't haul himself out. Finally, the girl's parents used pruning shears to cut the young man—his face as red as the roses—out of the prickly bush that was now decimated. Not a good way to meet a respectable girl's parents, but Gary still had enough alcohol in him to shrug off any embarrassment.

That night, despite being drunk, Gary impetuously decided to marry the girl, and within a short time, the knot was tied, although as it turned out, not too tightly. His new wife Julia quit school and got a job to help put Gary through college. But the alcohol continued to flow like an endless mountain stream, and the couple's relationship deteriorated into constant arguments. One night, in the dumps about his faltering marriage, Gary went to a friend's apartment, where marijuana was proffered to combat his despondency. "Total enlightenment," is how he describes the experience. "From that moment until I got sober," Gary confesses, "drugs were my best friend." He was hooked.

Soon, Gary came home one night and found everything he owned dumped on the front porch. Dazed, he picked it up, left, and didn't talk to his wife again for 20 years.

Gary had thought Julia was going to be a whole new life for him, and he was heartbroken. Alone and depressed, his drug use escalated. For a while, he lived with a Vietnam veteran who was dealing drugs, and Gary soon found buying and selling marijuana, heroin, and cocaine was an easy way to earn money for college tuition. It didn't take long to discover, though, "It is a lot easier to get into dealing than to get out of it."

Downtown Atlanta was a good place to deal—at least until Hell's Angels and the Outlaws took over. Rip-offs became commonplace, and Gary never knew with whom he was dealing. Violence, not brutal but bad, became a way of life. About the time the drug scene blew up on Peachtree, Gary ran—the old pattern of getting himself in a mess and then scampering to outrun the crisis. But the problems were always hot on his heels, threatening to engulf him.

Gary had attempted suicide before, and when he returned to his home area, he was so despondent he was ready to try again. Desperate for help, he called his old coach and paid him a visit. Pouring out his heart, Gary told the coach he didn't think he could live with some of the things he had done. A tortured soul himself (Gary had heard rumors his former coach had once killed a man), the coach told Gary, "You would be surprised at what a man can live with." Those words were enough to keep Gary going.

Having completed his college degree along the way in spite of his addiction, Gary taught school for a while, but he never gave up drugs. He smoked a couple of joints before and after school every day, and often, he would leave school at lunch to smoke another two or three. One night before a Parent-Teachers Association meeting, he stopped by a friend's house for "enlightenment" before the dull meeting. That evening, he got more than he bargained for—although he was at first reluctant, he let himself be persuaded to try LSD. Even spaced out, Gary knew his principal would be livid if he didn't show up, so he stumbled to school for the PTA meeting. What a sight he must have been—even if he hadn't been wobbling, his clothes were a clear sign to his principal something wasn't right: a wrinkled and tattered flag T-shirt and baggy pants patched in the crotch with an American flag. When Gary crawled under a table, mortified, that finished him. By morning, he was out of a job.

Next stop: radio. A good lifestyle for someone with a drinking/drug problem. Gary wasn't the only one addicted, and he and his associates regularly went behind the radio station to do drugs or drink. He also began playing in a church baseball league, but as usual, drinking gave him a short fuse, and his anger and rage spilled over everything he did.

Gary describes it like a "sponge filled with water so much that it drips water everywhere."

Gary raged at himself and others as he medicated himself to go to sleep and medicated himself to make it through each day. Anger consumed him—he calls it "sideways anger." Unable to understand anger and incapable of expressing it properly, people let it leak out sideways. In most cases, the fury hits the wrong target—someone who just happens to be in the wrong place at the wrong time, or someone who unknowingly triggers an explosion.

Hiding behind the anger are the known and unknown effects of addiction. "I had so many secrets," Gary remembers, acknowledging that all addiction is full of secrets. "It was like I had a hole in my stomach that was eating me up."

In 1979, he had an ACL reconstruction on his knee and was in a cast for six weeks. But his hospital stay didn't last long. The day after the surgery, a belligerent Gary kept demanding more and more pain medication, partly because he was in pain but also because he was in withdrawal. When he was refused, he demanded the nurses to call him a taxi, telling them, "I've got better dope at home!"

When the taxi driver got him home, the small black man who had helped him home from the hospital looked at the 70 steps he had to get Gary down to his basement apartment and knew they were in trouble. A young lady who lived in an upstairs apartment offered to help, and they finally made the descent. Before she left, she asked Gary if she could get him anything. He asked her if she would go pick up a case of Miller Lite for him. Eager to help, she agreed. When she returned, she once again asked if she could get anything for him. This time he sent her to a pharmacy to get him some Tylenol with Codeine. (Gary had a pharmacist friend who regularly gave him prescription drugs without prescriptions.) The next time the girl asked if she could get him anything else, he sent her to get him a pound of pot. Although she was hesitant, he convinced her it was alright. Two weeks later they married.

Gary's angel of mercy didn't stay around long. Two months into the marriage, the constant fighting and drug use took its toll, and she disappeared. It was the first time Gary tried to slash his wrists.

A few years later, Gary was still using and drinking. One night a friend called, needing to talk, but Gary was too high and told him it could wait until the next day. "The next morning," Gary recalls with tears threatening, "The boy's mother called and said he had killed himself." Devastated, overcome with remorse, Gary couldn't face life and he couldn't face people. He started arriving at the radio station every morning at 4:30 a.m. and managed to get some work done, but he took off before anyone else arrived around 7:30 a.m. At home, he refused to answer the phone or door. Heartsick about his friend, he couldn't forgive himself that he hadn't been there when he needed him.

Finally, the owner of the station forced Gary to meet with him, asking him what the problem was. Gary adamantly refused to tell him, but eventually the owner's persistence prevailed and Gary conceded, "I have—and have had for many years—a problem with drugs." Compassion sculpting his face, the owner came from behind his desk, hugged Gary, and told him, "I've known for a long time. We're going to get you some help." In denial, Gary resisted, declaring, "I'm not that bad. And I'm not going." The response? "Then you'll have to get another job." Two days later Gary entered treatment.

Gary admits his treatment didn't start well. He still had an attitude, as reflected by his responses to the questions on the interview sheet.

"How many drugs do you take on a daily basis?"

"A large amount."

"How many drugs do you take on a weekly basis?"

" Seven times a large amount."

"How many drugs do you take on a monthly basis?"

"Thirty times a large amount."

"I had a smart aleck mouth," Gary concedes with a little-boy grin. He didn't want to admit he had a problem, and he didn't want to be in treatment. It was only when the counselors told him he had a "disease" that he began to see his addiction for what it was.

"I had always felt I was a bad person trying to be good, not a sick person trying to get well," Gary asserts. He came to realize, "If addiction is treated like a disease, people get well. If it is treated like a sin, they keep drinking and/or taking drugs." For the first time, he saw how his father's drunkenness had been handled—his mother would call another pastor to come pray over his father. Treated like a sin, rather than an illness, his father's alcoholism got worse, not better.

Looking back, Gary says he now knows the true meaning of a statement he found in an Alcoholics Anonymous book: "God can do and will do things we can't do for ourselves."

When Gary entered treatment, he had no idea an FBI sting was about to come down and that he was facing two felony charges—two of 150 being handed down. Providentially, President Reagan had signed a law that a person in therapy cannot have his treatment interrupted, so the treatment center was not obligated to tell the FBI Gary was there. But the counselor did recommend that Gary contact the FBI when he finished treatment. Panicked by the legal consequences waiting for him, Gary threw himself into treatment, knowing it might be his only way out of the charges.

Today, Gary knows if God hadn't moved him toward treatment, he would likely have gone to jail. By the time he completed rehab 23 days later, the FBI had processed most of the warrants, and at that point Gary became "small potatoes." What he was being charged with was minor compared to the "big guys," who had all ratted on each other. Although Gary met with the FBI, he never heard from them again. "I escaped by the grace of God," he believes. And he knows now the only thing that kept him sober at that time was fear. He had come close to ruining his life forever—going to prison—and he feared God wouldn't bail him out again.

Ninety days later, when Gary received his red chip for three months of sobriety, it finally struck him: "God was doing something for me I couldn't do for myself." His mother and sister looked at him differently, and, for the first time in forever, he was proud of himself.

Gary returned to the radio station for a couple of weeks after his inpatient treatment, but he knew he couldn't stay in an environment where drugs and alcohol were so freely accepted and flowed so readily. He left to work at a local treatment center.

At first, Gary worried his friends wouldn't like him or want to be around him since he no longer did drugs, but recovery taught him what distinguishes friends: "Friends don't always understand, but they support you." Gary also learned not to judge others and to get angry at the behavior, not the person. And, when he started going to people he had hurt to make amends, he learned humility.

Over time, Gary learned that recovery is all about getting your behavior back within your value system. "I had to rebuild my self-esteem because I had acted outside my values so long. The most shaming thing, I finally discovered, is not to have done something bad but to keep doing things that hurt other people." Repeating the same behavior gives you the same results, Gary now knows. It's like his uncle once told him, "If you are wearing expensive alligator shoes and step in a mud puddle, you come into the house and clean them. Why would you want to go back outside and step in the same mud puddle again?"

Before he found sobriety, Gary used to compare himself to others and wonder if he could ever be "normal" again. Today he realizes that people he thought were "normal" are just like all humans. They resemble ducks who seem calm on the surface while paddling furiously beneath the water; on the surface they function, but others can't see how desperately they are struggling.

Recently, Gary shot a man during a home invasion. For a while, he had a hard time with what he had done. Even though the man was not killed, it reminded him that people respond differently to their fears. His mother and dad had acted out in violence, and he had learned that response. Fear set in when the robber started toward him, and he pulled the trigger four times. In shame, he rebuked himself, "I'm that same person I was before I went into treatment 27 years ago. I haven't changed." But he has. He had changed the behavior that was destroying him. Shooting a man in self-defense didn't change that. His bad behavior habits had been healed, and the Twelve Steps held him in good stead. Without them—without turning his problems over to God, Gary would have relapsed.

"God made me both good and bad," Gary says. "If I let God take care of the bad, the good will take care of itself."

Alcoholics Anonymous gave Gary three gifts, he states with firmness: "The first step helped me realize I was powerless over my addiction, and the second step assured me that there is a power greater than myself. If God could take care of my problems, why shouldn't I let him? In step three, I did that. These first three steps gave me peace of mind.

"Steps four through nine gave me peace of heart. I let go of the secrets in my heart. I admitted to myself and to another person what I had done and how I had felt. My guilt, my shame, my resentment, my anger, and my hopelessness poured out, cleansing my heart. And I tried to make amends. I grieved over things I had done that I hadn't been able to deal with when I was drugged.

"In the final steps, I found peace of soul. That came when I went to Russia to help open a couple of treatment centers after I had been sober 15 years. Helping others healed my spirit."

Today, his radiant smile highlighting his classic good looks, Gary is a successful banker who has been sober 27 years.

CHAPTER 15

FORGIVING YOURSELF AND MAKING AMENDS

It is in pardoning that we are pardoned.
SAINT FRANCIS OF ASSISI

The need for forgiveness most often starts with one or more hurts—hurts we endure from other people, hurts we inflict upon ourselves, or hurts we mete out to others. Hurts can send emotions free-falling into depression, throw them into a long-term battle with anger, or wreak havoc on relationships, leaving feelings of abandonment and aloneness.

Hurts become one of the biggest hang-ups in the addict's life. Before she can succeed in recovery, she must put past wrongs behind her. Words or actions that fill her with shame cannot be undone—but she doesn't have to let them haunt her.

While wiping the slate clean is not possible, forgiving herself, forgiving those who hurt her, and making amends with those she hurt, can free the addict to face the future.

FORGIVE YOURSELF

All of us see ourselves differently than we see others. As Gary discovered, "We are not good mirrors of ourselves. We can't see our goodness when we look at ourselves." Even with 27 years of sobriety, Gary adds, "The hardest person to forgive is yourself. I struggle with it constantly."

Forgiveness has to begin with "you," not "them." When an addict thinks he has ruined his life—and perhaps the lives of others—the guilt of his actions presses like an elephant's foot on his chest. Gripped by despair and hopelessness, he condemns himself. With drugs or alcohol, he could justify anything and everything; without a mind altered by chemicals, he feels the full brunt of the mess he has made of his life. Blaming himself keeps him shackled to the past, preventing the focus he needs on his future.

The biggest driver of hopelessness is an addict's feeling that he is unworthy and unlovable. Monteleone tells a patient who feels hopeless that the only requirement to have value is to breathe. Self-esteem has a "doing piece"— in other words, a person must accomplish something to have self-esteem. Self-worth, on the other hand, requires only to be alive—"Our worthiness comes from the higher power who gave us life. Addicts who feel unworthy must move from feeling like a 'human doing' who doesn't measure up to being a 'human being.' To be valued requires an unconditional love principle," Monteleone contends, adding, "we all have that from our higher power."

Unconditional love applies to self as well as to others significant in our lives. Monteleone says the lack of self-forgiveness equates to self-hatred. As an example, she tells about a patient who felt responsible for his brother's overdose and death. The brothers were both addicted, but the surviving brother couldn't forgive himself because he had obtained drugs for his brother the night he died. "He had an incredible need to ask his brother for forgiveness," Monteleone recalls, "but it wasn't possible to go to him so he had to forgive himself."

Monteleone notes, "On some level, all recovering addicts have to deal with forgiveness. Most people don't walk into treatment centers because they have decided they want to recover—they come because a trigger compels them to seek help; for example, multiple DUIs mount up, a family member leaves, a job is lost, or some other catastrophic event occurs, all consequences of the addiction." Monteleone emphasizes, "If there are no consequences, addicts don't see the need for treatment; the desire necessary for recovery is absent. But when a person hurts himself or others and keeps doing it, he begins to beat up on himself. When the next trigger is pulled, he may be motivated to seek help."

No addict is the first or the last to make life-changing mistakes. As Alexander Pope said, "To err is human." Everyone misses the mark. The shame the recovering person feels may be deserved, but it shouldn't be a life sentence. He has paid the price for his addiction in what he has lost, whether a job, a loved one, or something else.

Hope emanates from the second half of Alexander Pope's statement: "To forgive is divine." Even in deep despair, the addict finds grace when he admits the wrongness of his ways and seeks light in the darkness of his life. When a person accepts divine forgiveness, the key to peace is to stop stumbling on remorse.

Punishing himself when a divine being has pardoned the addict is foolish. Beating himself up doesn't change the past; he should accept forgiveness and enjoy the peace of grace. Thomas Aquinas told us, "The splendor of a soul in grace is so seductive that it surpasses the beauty of all created things." Grace is amazing, whether from above or within a person.

FORGIVE THOSE WHO HAVE HURT YOU

Restoring relationships torn asunder by hurts that contributed to an addict's being hooked may or may not happen. If the person who made her vulnerable to addiction recognizes the wrongs and asks for forgiveness, she should accept the olive branch and attempt to restore a positive relationship. This may not be easy—the hurts may run so deep and be so tender that she doesn't want to let go of her anger and resentment. But she can choose to let love be stronger than hate. It may not happen overnight, but she can learn to love again, letting forgiveness grow in her heart like a reborn iris as she works through recovery.

What does the recovering person do if those who hurt her don't accept their responsibility for the pain they caused? For years, she has held deep-seated bitterness that someone she loved wounded her emotionally—or perhaps physically. To cleanse the wound, she wants to hear the person say he is sorry. If that doesn't happen, she has two choices: Allow the person to control her thoughts by continuing to feel the hurt, or refuse to allow the hurts to persist in maiming her emotions. Hatred hurts the hater more than it hurts the hated. Hanging on to hurts is a horrendous burden—and it is one the recovering addict doesn't have to bear. Resentment and hate eat away at a person's insides, keeping her in an emotional turmoil. A person in recovery should forgive those who have hurt her, not so much for them as for herself.

In *Faces of Grief*, Hoppe tells the story of one man who demonstrated a divinely inspired way of dealing with the person who hurt him. "Pope John Paul II walked into a prison and said to Mehmet Ali Agca, the hired assassin who had tried to kill him, 'I forgive you.' Shot as he rode in an open car across St. Peter's Square on a late spring day in 1981, the Pope took two hits to his stomach, one to his right arm, and one to his left hand. After emergency surgery saved his life, he visited Agca in Rebibbia Prison in Italy; and, in a moment of extraordinary grace, held the hand that shot him and forgave the would-be killer. In that instant, the violence of St. Peter's Square was transformed into peace and pardon." So, too, must addicts accept the agony and harm inflicted by others, understanding them as part of life's misfortunes and finding a way to absolve them.

MAKE AMENDS WITH THOSE YOU HAVE HURT

Atonement literally means the making of reparation for doing wrong. Although difficult, this requires hands-on work. The addict should make a list of the people he hurt and come up with a plan for how he will attempt to make amends. The best way is to meet with the person privately to acknowledge the wrong and ask for forgiveness. If that isn't possible, he might write him a letter. If possible, he should also make restitution. If he stole from someone, he should pay it back if he can, even if it takes years. If that is not possible, then a sincere apology may be the best he can offer.

Occasionally, one or more persons the addict injured may not be willing to grant forgiveness. Their hurt may be too deep-rooted or too raw, or perhaps it is impossible for them to understand and accept how addiction affects actions. It is not the addict's burden to make others forgive him— his job is to ask. He is only responsible for what he does, not how the other person responds. It may be awkward or even heartbreaking if the other person isn't ready to forgive, but the addict must accept where that person is emotionally. After Sylvia completed treatment and had begun a life of sobriety, she wrote letters to the person from whom she had stolen and to the managing partner of the firm, as well as to the person who had helped her obtain the job and to a friend within the company. None acknowledged her letters, although the managing partner did assist in getting charges against her dropped. Still, not receiving a response after she had opened her heart with candor and in genuine remorse cut deeply.

If a person has been hurt repeatedly, he may not be willing to trust that the addict is sincere—that she will not hurt them again by her actions, especially by relapsing. One of Sylvia's daughters had a difficult time trusting her again after her final relapse, but eventually the breach was mended and a strong, positive familial relationship has been restored. Time and consistency healed the fractured relationship. If a person's own relationships are not as quick in mending, she should stay committed to recovery by refocusing her life on the future and by not giving up hope that reconciliation is possible.

CHAPTER 16

UNHOOKED AND HOPEFUL:

Keith's Personal Story

Keith had it all—he grew up in a near-perfect family, completed college, married a beautiful girl who gave him a little boy he cherished, and co-founded a granite business when he was just 25 years old. At 28, his income was six figures, and life was good. Or, so it seemed on the surface before his world came crashing down when his partner did some digging in the company books and found Keith had been pilfering money—big money. Faced with felony charges or being forced out of the business, Keith chose to give up all rights to the company he had built from the ground up. A dramatic wake-up call.

What no one knew until that happened—even his wife and parents—was that Keith had a secret drug life that had rendered him conscienceless. The craving for pills drove him to abandon his value system to get what he had to have. Obtaining the drugs was all that mattered; how he got them was immaterial. He didn't want to betray his partner, but in his altered state of thinking, if that was what it took, so be it. "It was all about me," Keith concedes.

It hadn't started out that way. When he drank his first bottle of liquor in the family's basement at the age of 12 or 13, he had no idea his DNA was hard-wired for vulnerability to addiction. He just liked the buzz and relived it repeatedly as he partied his way through high school and college. By his early 20s, he started doing cocaine, and then he tried Percocet. He was hooked instantly. Until then, he had his liquor and drugs, and no doubt he was addicted, but the Percocet took him to a new level from which there was no return. Pain pills became his drug of choice, and he developed a network of about 15 dealers who happily supplied him, given that he had the money. And, as long as he could function at work, that wasn't a problem—at least until his daily cravings weren't satisfied with less than 1000 mg. of Oxycontin, an 8-ball of cocaine, and 30 or so beers. At fifty cents a milligram, his Oxycontin needs alone took $500 a day. The cocaine added another tidy sum. The beer costs were minor compared to the drugs, but the total for everything was astronomical. He was making good money from his business, but not that good. That's when he started "cooking the books," selling granite for cash behind his partner's back.

Keith's family life was far from ideal, but as long as his wife didn't realize how badly he was hooked, the home fires kept burning. He would function fairly normally at work (or at least he thought he was acting appropriately), but after a few hours of pills and alcohol at night, he was stoned. His wife knew he drank a lot of beer, yet for a long time she never suspected he was doing drugs. One time, unable to keep his shame from penetrating his struggling spirit, he started going to a methadone clinic. When his wife found a business card about the clinic in his billfold, she was furious he hadn't told her but was convinced he was on the right path to recover. A nurse, she knew that methadone clinics monitored the blood for other drugs, so she believed as long as he kept going, he could stay unhooked. What she didn't know was that Keith failed every drug test. Like many unscrupulous methadone facilities, the clinic kept giving Keith the medication despite confirming he was on other drugs. He was as hooked on methadone as he was on his drugs of choice, but he says at least it was easier to eventually give up the methadone.

Today, as Keith candidly shares his story, he doesn't look like a "dope head." The ruggedly handsome young man with a tousled mane of brown hair looks like the kid next door. His azure blue eyes hide nothing, and his beautiful smile is captivating. Innocent and alluring, he sits relaxed, knowing he has nothing to hide. He's made the transition from a secret life to an open book.

After losing his company, Keith almost lost his wife and young son. "Never again," she warned. And he believed her. But that wasn't all that motivated him to enter a residential treatment center. He was tired of what pills were doing to him. "It was excruciating to wake up and know you had to find 1000 mg. of Oxycontin every day," he recalls with a grin that is almost a grimace. Disgusted with himself and sick of his daily foraging for pills, he says, "I had no choice but to make the right choice— get help." Although withdrawal was awful (made worse because Keith wasn't honest about how much alcohol he was consuming in addition to the drugs), the newfound sense of freedom Keith felt from not being dependent on drugs was so powerful he wonders aloud why anyone would ever go back on drugs once they are unhooked. "I was a shell of who I used to be. I didn't like who I was—I didn't feel 'normal,' so why would I want to return to that life?" he questions.

Unlike the majority of addicts, Keith never looked back. Off drugs and alcohol for the first time in ten years, with a clear mind he discerned the buzz wasn't worth the turmoil stemming from the side effects of the drugs. "The drugs dictate your lifestyle. I got the message," he declares emphatically.

Intuitively, Keith knows his brain is wired to turn the addiction button on with only one drink or one pill. Once he exposed himself to alcohol and drugs, it was a one-way street. Today, he knows the path would have become a dead end if he had not made a U-Turn. He also recognizes the only way to stay on the street of recovery is never to let the hook get near his mouth.

Keith has been in recovery for two years, and he's adamantly committed to staying there. His marriage was rocky for a while, but it's getting better every day. His wife, now studying to be a nurse practitioner, not only acknowledges that addiction is a disease but also that the decision to stay clean is solely her husband's. He's going to do what he's going to do whether she trusts him or not, so she doesn't constantly badger him about relapsing. Instead, she's there for him when he needs her. And, she's given him another darling little boy. More incentive to stay unhooked.

Although Keith grew up in a religious family, he says he still struggles with the concept of a higher power. But NA did help him understand addiction—that it is as much an illness as cancer. He learned not to be ashamed to call himself an addict. "Healing came from knowledge," he asserts. "Learning how my brain was wired helped me realize I am not a bad person."

Keith says he is "not big on looking backward." Forgiving himself wasn't difficult because he internalized that the alcohol and drugs controlled his irrational thoughts and bad actions. What he did when he was high wasn't who he really is. As for the NA dictum to make amends, he thinks the best way to do that is to be the way he used to be. "The best apology is just to live a good life." And he's doing that.

Like Sylvia, Keith hasn't stayed consistent with attendance at recovery groups. He did the "90 meetings in 90 days" recommended by his treatment facility, and he still goes once a month or so. But he doesn't believe group meetings are the key to his continued recovery. That comes from within—from wanting to be a good husband and father, from wanting to be in control of his life. "You have to want recovery yourself," he avows. He doesn't need to be motivated by what others say at meetings. "To be free from the obsession for drugs is the best feeling in the world."

Even though Keith doesn't follow all of the NA tenets, he is quick to say he admires people who do. When he has a friend in trouble, he doesn't hesitate—he recommends the treatment center that opened the door to his new life. The Twelve Step program used there—and in most treatment centers—works. It just works in different ways for different people.

Today, at 30 years of age, Keith is back in the stone business. He's not the owner or boss anymore, and that's okay for now. The two owners of the company for which he works are both recovering addicts themselves, and they understand where he has been and where he is going. The three-way support system among the men works.

Keith has come a long way from the hot, sultry day in July 2009 when his world collapsed. He works extra jobs to reach the income level he had as a partner in his old company, but he's alright with that. The same obsessive personality that hooked him on drugs is a positive driver in the world of work. His priorities are in order, and listening to him, there is no doubt he knows where he is in life and likes it. Unhooked and hopeful.

CHAPTER 17

STAYING IN RECOVERY

We must all suffer from one of two pains: the pain of discipline or the pain of regret. The difference is discipline weighs ounces while regret weighs tons.

JOHN ROHN

Rohn's quote gives strong motivation for staying in recovery—following through with the addict's commitment may be challenging; but if he relapses, the regret will create a heavier burden. Yet, willpower, which is nothing more than discipline, alone is not enough. Monteleone reminds us, "The thinking and behavior links cannot be controlled when a part of the brain is demanding more alcohol or opiates to survive." She compares the difficulty to creating a track through a muddy field with a wagon. "After the mud dries and hardens," she declares, "it is almost impossible to drive through the field without going in the ruts." She adds, "In human terms, an addict may not even be aware of his behavior and thoughts—he just moves based on his compulsions."

For addicts trying to stay off the hook, the average rate of relapse within three months is more than 60 percent. Undoubtedly, all of them wanted to stay sober.

Stopping may well be the easiest part, for as Mark Twain observed, "It's easy to stop smoking...I've done it hundreds of times." Staying stopped—whether from cigarettes or any other substance—is the hard part.

Unfortunately, most addicts, as well as people in their support systems, do not want to talk about the possibility of relapse. To utter the word "relapse" implies failure is inevitable, but it is not. A relapse is just one more bump in the road to recovery. If the addict can avoid the pothole, great. If he hits it, after the stumble he simply starts again.

Al, whose story is told in the next chapter, reminds those struggling that "It's work, but it gets better. If I can do this, you can." Al keeps going to meetings not just for himself, but also because he wants to help others stay unhooked.

Al also concedes, "I don't know how you can get anybody sober or clean—you probably can't." But he is quick to add, "You and God have a fighting chance; alone, you can't do it. It's a daily thing. It never goes away."

An analogy, author unknown, illustrates options available when adversity strikes.

It starts with a few carrots, a couple of eggs, and coffee and was shared by a mother with her daughter, who complained about her hard life. Tired of fighting and struggling, it seemed that as soon as one problem was solved, another arose. The daughter appeared ready to give up.

Walking into the kitchen, the mother filled three pots with water and placed each on high on the gas burners of her stove. When the water boiled, the woman placed carrots in one pot, eggs in another, and in the last one she placed ground coffee beans. Silently, she stood and watched the pots continue boiling.

Twenty minutes later, the woman turned off the burners. She dipped the carrots up, fished the eggs out, and ladled the coffee—placing each in a separate bowl. Turning to her daughter, she asked, "Tell me, what do you see?"

The daughter replied with a quizzical look, "Just carrots, eggs, and coffee." But when her mother brought her closer and asked her to feel the carrots, she noted they were soft. The mother then asked her to take the eggs and crack the shell, releasing hard-boiled eggs. Finally, the mother asked the daughter to taste the coffee wafting its rich aroma in the air.

Mystified, the daughter asked, "What does it mean, mother?"

In simple terms, the mother explained that each of the objects had faced the same adversity—boiling water—but each reacted differently. The carrot went in strong, hard and unrelenting, but after being subjected to the boiling water, it softened and became weak.

The egg started out fragile, its thin outer shell protecting its liquid interior. After sitting in the boiling water, its inside became hardened.

The ground coffee beans were unique—after they were in the boiling water, they had changed the water.

The addict should ask himself, "Which am I? A carrot that seems strong but with pain and adversity becomes soft and loses its strength? Or, am I like the egg that starts with a malleable heart but hardens with the heat? Did I have a fluid spirit, but after the trials of my life, become hardened and stiff? Does my shell look the same, but on the inside am I bitter and tough with a stiff spirit and a hardened heart?

"Or, am I like the coffee bean, changing the hot water, the very circumstance that brings the pain, releasing its fragrance and flavor?"

If the addict is like the coffee bean, when life is at its worst, he will get better and change the situation around him. When the hours are the darkest and trials are their greatest, the addict must ask himself, "Can I color the circumstances with my attitude?" When adversity strikes, a cup of coffee can be a good reminder.

SUGGESTIONS TO HELP THE RECOVERY PROCESS

Chapter 3 identified factors affecting relapse, as well as triggers and stages, so those will not be repeated here, but we offer a number of suggestions that may help the recovery process.

The best way to stay in recovery is to keep recovery as the number one priority. Do not let problems, responsibilities, or activities interfere with the commitment. Attend recovery meetings and keep a support system active. Regularly interacting with others in recovery reinforces the addict's own commitment and demonstrates that recovery is possible.

Monteleone says support for the addict who wants to recover is huge—a must. She describes addicts as 3-legged stools. "Early in recovery a substance abuser is a one-legged stool, and he can't stand alone. Even if the person gains a second leg in treatment, she will still wobble and fall if she doesn't have the third leg—a support system."

A support group is a safe haven where a person can share his or her experiences and find others who have similar experiences. As an illustration, Monteleone notes, "Auschwitz survivors had a terrible time getting over their experiences at the death camp until they were brought together and shared their feelings and experiences." She avers the same principle applies to addicts.

Monteleone believes, "The best anti-drug is a healthy relationship." Addicts who develop healthy relationships, she says, are survivors. Those relationships can be with other members of a support group, a church group, or a family. Healthy relationships require that a person be able to go inside himself and find his emotions and express them. This involves social skills to navigate a person's world with other people. In effect, Monteleone says, "Isolation leads to regression. Relationships lead to progress."

The core message for addicts, Monteleone reaffirms, is that "the way out of addiction is through healthy relationships." Addiction disconnects people from themselves and others. The recovering addict must constantly examine himself, his lifestyle, and his set of skills, asking, "What am I doing that may not contribute to my welfare or the welfare of others?" In other words, "How can I be healthier?"

Other suggestions for staying in recovery:

- When feeling lonely or down, connect with people in your recovery group, especially your sponsor, or with family or friends. Even after 28 years of sobriety, Gary A knows where to find people who understand—in NA or AA groups. The key is to refuse to sit at home and brood, feeling sorry for yourself. Get out and do something with someone—occupying your time occupies your mind, keeping it from dwelling on your aloneness. Still, spend enough time in solitude to stay in touch with your inner being.

- When faced with problems, keep them in perspective. Don't overreact, but don't ignore them either. And, don't go into a "worst case scenario" panic. Whenever possible, talk about the problem with someone you trust. Consider all alternatives and their consequences, then determine the best way to deal with the issue. Break the solution down into manageable steps before taking action. From experience, Terry C knows that every time he deals with a problem rationally, his recovery muscle grows stronger.

- When conflicts arise with friends or family members, keep emotions under control. Pause and take a deep breath before responding. And, when the confrontation is over, let it go. Do not let it eat away at you, rehashing what you said or wished you had said. Conflicts are a part of the ebb and flow of life, but they do not have to control how you feel. You can choose to be upset, or you can choose not to be upset. While you can't control the other person's actions or words, you can control how you respond to them emotionally. Albert Ellis, a psychotherapist, suggested that you say something like this to yourself: "He [or she] may choose to be difficult, but I choose not to be upset."

Terry recalls one conflict where he first chose to be upset but then chose otherwise. It happened after about eight or nine months of sobriety. Working part-time in a restaurant, his boss jumped him one night because he undercooked a piece of chicken. Infuriated, Terry tried to convince his boss the chicken was done enough. When his boss cut the chicken open and proved his allegation, Terry says, "It flew all over me, and I stalked out the door. I wanted to go get drunk." He sat on the steps of his apartment for a while, wanting to call someone but he didn't have a phone. Finally, someone came up and he borrowed a phone to call a friend in management at CADAS.

"Janet," he whined, "I really want to go get drunk."

"Well," Janet responded, almost flippantly, "why don't you just go get drunk?"

Terry's response, which began by calling Janet a not-so-nice name which he thankfully said to himself and not to Janet, ended with "How dare you say that?"

But then he thought, "I don't have to get drunk. In fact, nothing in my life is so bad that a drink or a drug won't make it worse. All the good things in my life I now cherish won't be any better with a drink or a pill."

Janet's challenge forced Terry to face whether drinking and drugs would help or hurt his life.

- Be honest—consistently. If you habitually tell little fibs, it becomes easy to tell big ones, leading to cover-ups and denials. Acknowledge mistakes as a way of life. Don't deny culpability for your actions. Although it wasn't easy, being truthful with his parents and with others he had wronged made Terry feel better about himself.

- Avoid high-risk situations, especially if your emotions are already on edge. Plan in advance how you will deal with a situation that might cause you to have cravings.

- Engage in activities that relieve stress. Exercise is especially helpful—join a gym, participate in sports, or just walk in the open air of your neighborhood.

- Don't be overconfident, thinking, "There is no way I'll ever start using again" or "I'm now strong enough I can take one pill or one drink and stop." Confidence is good, but denying vulnerability is dangerous. As an addict, you must always be on the alert. Al stresses that the second year is worse than the first. "Everybody was patting you on the back, telling you how proud they were of you, the first year. The second year is when you have to focus doubly hard on maintaining your commitment."

- Monitor and evaluate your emotional stresses. If you are hurt, tired, angry, or disappointed, deal with your feelings rather than repress them. As noted above, talking with someone helps—it can be cathartic, letting you get strong or negative feelings out of your system. Terry C has found that every time he deals with fear or other negative emotions, he grows stronger as a person, gaining a little more hope.

- Learn humility in the sense described by the Reverend Joseph J. Gallagher: "...humility consists less in thinking little of yourself than in thinking of yourself little." Focus on the needs of others more than you focus on yours.

- Live in the present and plan for the future. Assess your life as it is today, not what it might have been. Accept where you are and decide where you want to be tomorrow, and be prepared that you won't get there overnight. Take life slowly, and live for the moment. No one has a guarantee about tomorrow, and life is too short to waste today. For Terry C, family and his creative work fill days, and he's not about to waste even one of them. Temptation is not an issue because even a glass of wine with a meal is not worth the risk. He has a four-year-old and a seven-year-old depending on him.

WHOLENESS

Developing a new way of life takes time, commitment, and practice. Spirituality can serve as a powerful buttress to an addict's efforts. In *The Unsettling of America*, Wendell Berry advised that a man can be made whole by comprehending his place in the whole of creation. Spiritual studies, prayer, and meditation will help a person find her way through the blizzard of life with a sense of wholeness. Sometimes that wholeness seems hidden in a whiteout, but it is always there.

Wholeness does not require perfection. Instead, Palmer (2004) tells us that wholeness entails embracing brokenness as a basic facet of life. When we live divided lives—compartmentalizing our spirituality far away from the behaviors that cause us angst—we sacrifice this wholeness. When we take the broken pieces of our lives and let the light of our spirituality shine on them, we see truth and hope. Only then can the fragments of our life be molded together into a whole being—a vessel that may have cracks but still has beauty and holds the water of life.

One way to nurture the spirit is to spend time in nature. Among snow-capped mountains, in flower-strewn valleys, on banks of rushing rivers and shores of turbulent oceans, we can see the small place we hold in the intricate design of the universe. The key to recovery is to hold tight and appreciate this unique place, however significant or insignificant it may be.

Psalm 139:13-14 says we were knit together in our mother's womb and that we are fearfully and wonderfully made..., concluding that the soul knows that very well. A person's soul is his grounding rod, keeping him rooted to his core beliefs. If a person stays in touch with his soul, he will stay in recovery.

CHAPTER 18

UNHOOKED AND HOPEFUL:

Al E's Personal Story

m eeting Al for the first time, one would never suspect he spent most of his life hooked on alcohol and drugs. Easy-going and laid back with a smile that sneaks up on you, he seems content with life. Laughter comes spontaneously, lighting his eyes and leaving them with a twinkle after the merriment fades when he tells about his journey through the river of addiction. At 52, he's found peace, and it shows.

Al grew up in a good family, but he never quite fit in. As a child, he was captivated by Otis on the *Andy Griffith Show*; everybody loved Otis, who was always good for a laugh, and Al ate that up. He also looked up to Dean Martin, who had such a good time drinking. In Al's young mind, a connection clicked: Drinking meant having fun. In the sixth grade, he decided to see if the equation was real. One day he slipped into a store near his grade school, stole some malt liquor, and headed to a nearby drainage ditch. With a little buzz in his head, he thought he had a glorious career ahead. Looking back, with a big guffaw, he says, "Here I was, drinking hot malt liquor in a drainage ditch, and I thought I had the world at my feet."

Al liked the buzz, so he repeated his drainage ditch exercise a couple more times. Then, at different friends' homes, if there was liquor in the house, he'd suggest he and his buddies have a bit. (There was never any liquor in Al's home, so he had to get it someplace else.) Getting a nip here and there satisfied him for the next few years, but at age 15, he began buying liquor at J.D. Liquors in downtown Chattanooga, Tn. Back then, they didn't "card" you, and Al was tall enough to look older than he was. The more he drank, the more he wanted. During high school, at lunch he would duck out of the cafeteria and run to his car, where he kept a bottle of Jim Beam. "It made me feel good," he remembers, and he was smart enough to cover up his noon forays. Hickory Farms made a liquor-flavored candy, so if anyone ever asked him if he had been drinking, he'd pull one of the candies from his pocket, and say, "Of course not, I've been sucking on this candy."

Al concedes he was probably an alcoholic by the time he graduated from high school. A quart would last him about two days. Ole Otis and Dean Martin had set a good example—they were right: drinking equaled fun. Before he made it out of high school, a little too much fun left him with a pregnant girlfriend—by the time he enrolled at Auburn University, he was married. Knowing he had a family to support, Al went to school year-round and worked on the side. But the more responsible he felt, the more stress he had, and with work, school, a wife, and a new baby, he didn't have time to sleep. Alcohol didn't help with that problem, so he added amphetamines. They transformed him into superman. He didn't have to worry anymore; he could handle all of the balls he was juggling. He skimmed over the surface and made it through his bachelor's degree with flying colors—assuring his acceptance into pharmacy school.

If undergraduate school took a few pills to survive, professional school took a few more. No problem—in pharmacy school he had easy access to all he needed. With a few pills and a bright mind, he did it again, making it through a tough degree despite his heavy work schedule and increasing problems at home. With a crooked grin, he says, "My wife didn't have a drug problem, but she did have an infidelity one." She stayed with him until he finished pharmacy school and a little longer after that, and then she hit the road, leaving their two-month-old and four-year-old sons with their daddy.

Cunningly, Al thought, "Now I have a reason to drink. Poor, pitiful me." He was trying to study for state boards while changing diapers, dealing with colic, and working at a hospital to support his sons. The only way he could stay up all day after being up most of the night was to use cocaine. At night, he drank liquor—to the tune of three or four half gallons a week.

Al didn't know if he was running away from something or running to something, but he couldn't seem to settle in one place. Over the next year, he moved from Montgomery to Selma to Huntsville, Al., trying to get a grip, thinking, "In another town, I can start over and put all this behind me." But it just got worse. When he hit rock bottom in Huntsville, he knew he was about to crash and burn. A seizure while he was working at a drug store gave his secret away, and he lost his pharmacy license. Telling this, Al shakes his head in disbelief, adding, "I had only had my license a year."

Desperate, he called his parents and went home, two young children in tow. They were shocked and dismayed at how Al looked—he had lost 80 pounds. Back in his hometown, Al had no access to drugs, but he still drank heavily. Determined to get his pharmacy license back, he worked at a supermarket, sweeping floors, changing light bulbs, and whatever, trying to get his foot in the door of the grocery-store pharmacy.

In 1983, Al appeared before the licensing board to plead his case. Nervous, he had a few drinks before he went in, and one of the board members asked him if he had had anything to drink to calm his nerves. Reluctantly, Al admitted he had. Surprisingly, the board member responded, "That was probably a good idea." In the interview with the licensing board, Al recalls no one asked him if he had been in treatment. It was almost as if they just said, "Here you go, here's your license. Now be a good boy."

License back in hand, Al returned to the supermarket where he had been a model employee (no one had any idea he had been drinking on the job) and was rewarded with a job in the pharmacy. He continued to drink and began to take a few hydrocodones and amphetamines home each night to combat ongoing foot pain. On the surface, he was functioning fairly normally, but inside he was paddling hard to stay afloat. His mind altered, he made another bad marriage choice that didn't last long.

Surprisingly, though he drank every night, his two sons didn't realize their father was an alcoholic. They had never seen him any other way, so they thought nothing about the way he acted after a few drinks. Still, he tried not to drink before he went to ballgames with them, but he made sure they saw him early in the game, hoping they wouldn't notice if he had to slip out and have a drink.

Even though his kids were oblivious to their dad's increasing dependence, Al knew he was getting in deeper and deeper. He used any inane excuse he could find to justify putting chemicals in his system. And, he used the same convoluted thinking about the drugs he was stealing from the pharmacy where he worked. "I came in early today," or "They don't pay me for all the extra work I do," or whatever—it didn't take much to push down his jumpy conscience.

When he met Liz, his third wife (who was also a pharmacist) at the hospital where they both worked, Al knew he wanted to get unhooked. Looking back, he candidly admits the first two times he married it was for the wrong reason. The first time, he married because his girlfriend was pregnant. The second time, he married because he thought having a mother would be good for his kids. But the third time, he married because he couldn't live without the woman with whom he had fallen in love.

The worst part of the early days of Al's third marriage was having to lie to his wife. "It just about killed me," he says, his voice still filled with pain at the memory of his duplicity. But he didn't know what to do. When he tried to quit, the shakes drove him back to more alcohol or another hydrocodone. "I felt miserable about deceiving Liz," Al says with regret, "but I convinced myself I was doing the best I could."

Life was like playing charades. Guess who Al is. He no longer knew himself—not only with Liz, but also with his kids.

On the job, Al learned to stay one step ahead. When he sensed he was under suspicion, he would resign and find another job. Once, though, when he had had too much to drink before coming to work and his boss confronted him, accusing him of stealing drugs, Al told her she was a lying slut. He then started to argue, but the look in her eye told him it was useless—he hadn't moved on fast enough this time.

But it was worse than just losing another job: Ninety-three counts of felony theft. Forget that he had a legitimate foot problem that required pain medication. No one bought that he needed as much pain medicine as he was stealing—and if he did, it was still theft. The vicious cycle of getting caught by Liz, making up lies, cutting back, and then going back deep into drugs was over. The quantity of drugs involved warranted calling in DEA (Drug Enforcement Agency), and they weren't interested in hearing why he was on drugs. They just wanted to get him out of the pharmacy. He could go to jail or go to treatment. An easy choice, Al thought. "I can do this. I lost my license once and got it back. I can do this." And, at that point, his game plan was to use the one that had scored last time. Cut back just enough to fool everyone. Tell the counselors what they want to hear.

The authorities gave Al a choice of two treatment centers. One told him the minimum treatment program was three months. Cornerstone of Knoxville said he could be out in as little as 28 days, although some people stayed in the program up to a year. Putting his persuasive charm in motion, Al told Liz the Cornerstone program was the right one for him. All the while, Al was telling anyone who would listen that the DEA was exaggerating. In his head, he reasoned, "I'll be fine. I'm just going up there to nod my head, fool them, and get my license back."

Off Al goes to Knoxville. Of course, before he got out of Chattanooga he stopped and bought a bottle of liquor. "Like a dope," he says, "I drank all the way to Knoxville." By the time he got there, he was so drunk he couldn't find Cornerstone. He called his wife to tell her he was lost, probably hoping she would tell him to just come back home, but he detected a firmness in her voice he hadn't heard before. "Just find it, Al." And he did.

Staggering into Cornerstone, Al slammed his fist on the reception counter. By now, he had enough alcohol in his system to be downright cocky. Crazily, he thought within a day or two the whole pharmacy industry would descend on Cornerstone and demand his release. Delusional, Al once again thought the world was at his feet. He wasn't really drunk—and he certainly wasn't an alcoholic. Well, maybe there were some folks there who were; maybe he could help them.

Cornerstone employees had seen all kinds of people walk through their door, but when Al walked in with a big glass of liquor in his hand, it was a first. Everyone in the building came running. Al couldn't understand what all the commotion was about. What was the big deal—surely they didn't expect him to stop drinking before he checked himself in. Not quite ready to give up his glass, he argued he should be able to keep it until he was fully enrolled in the program. Shaking her head, the intake counselor started by asking him if he had had a drink that day and then caught herself, saying, "I think we can skip that one." Moving to the next part of the intake process, she pulled a breathalyzer from her desk. But then she glanced at it and said, "We'll bypass this today." Evidently, a person could score too high to be admitted.

Al doesn't remember much about the next few days. He knows he had the shakes a lot, and he remembers telling the attendants he didn't want anything to help. "The quicker I get through this," he thought, "the quicker I can get out of here and get something to calm my nerves."

After the first few days, Al remembers being herded into the "druggy buggy" to go to an AA meeting. He also recalls he had to sit in a chair with arms—otherwise, he would have bounced right out of the chair from shaking so hard.

Other than that, Al's memory is sketchy. He knows he felt strung out, but he wanted to fill out the forms the staff gave him. Confident he could snow the counselors, he poured it on as he expounded on the first step—admitting powerlessness over alcohol. "I wrote exactly what I knew they wanted to hear," Al says. "I thought it was so beautiful the person reading it might cry." In the group meeting that evening, everyone told him how wonderful his response was; pats on the back convinced him he had pulled off his intended con job. "This is easy," he thought to himself. "They'll probably let me out in 28 days."

The next day, a counselor brought a stack of papers and told Al he needed to complete them. Looking askance at the counselor, Al didn't understand until he read the heading on the first page: "First Step for the Client Who Thinks He Knows Everything."

"They were on to me," Al says with a grimace. I thought, "They are going to cut me off at the knees."

After completing the stack of papers that seemed like it was a foot high, Al moved on to the second step: "We came to believe that a Power greater than ourselves could restore us to sanity." Explaining his confusion at this point, Al says, "Growing up, every Sunday morning my parents got me ready, clipped on my little tie, and I went to Sunday School. I could tell you about Daniel, Paul, and Samuel; but I didn't have any more personal relationship with them than I did with the historical figures—Caesar, Napoleon, etc.—I had read about."

The second step was hard for Al—he believed in God, but he struggled with where he fit into the big picture. He argued with one man, "I'm just a little addict; God doesn't have time for me." But his fellow patient told him repeatedly, "You are as important to God as Adam, as Moses. He doesn't play favorites." Al tried to let that sink it, but he wasn't convinced. So when he got to step three ("We made a decision to turn our will and our lives over to the care of God as we understood Him."), he balked. Free of mind-altering drugs and alcohol, he had his wits about him, so he started arguing again. He wanted someone to define "decision," "will," and "life." But he didn't like the definitions. He tried his own definition of life on for size: "Life is what happens while you are making other plans." A junkie from Chicago, innocent as a newborn lamb, said, "That's beautiful—that should be a song. Maybe we could get John Lennon to sing it for us." Crestfallen, Al knew he had been exposed again. "Little by little, they were chipping away at me," he says softly.

But Al was adamant. "I am not going to turn my will over; it's my life." At that time, Christmas was about two to three weeks away, and the counselors were trying to get everyone into the Christmas spirit. Everyone was decorating, having fun—except Al. When the counselor told him, "This will be a good Christmas; be glad you are here," Al was ready to sucker punch him. "I'm not going to do it. This is going to be the worst Christmas ever. You can't make me enjoy it."

Liz came up that week for "Family Fundamentals," a weekly time for families to meet with patients and try to work through home issues. It was "put up or shut up" time, but Al wasn't ready to play. Liz told how Al had been at home, especially how much he had lied to her, and Al admitted it was true. But he wasn't gracious about it. In fact, he was flat mad at having to tell the world what a liar he had been. He tried to bait Liz, but she wasn't biting.

In a quiet voice, Liz explained she had gone to church the previous weekend, even though she had had to work on Sunday. When Al had been at home, they went to church regularly except when they had Sunday shifts. Then, they stayed at home because it was too much of a rush to go and make it to work on time. For some reason, Liz kept feeling she should go to church that morning, but she resisted. After coffee, she once again had the feeling she needed to go to the worship service. She finally gave in, she told Al, and when she heard the sermon, she was glad she had. Then she handed him a CD of the sermon, telling Al she had not told the pastor Al was in treatment until after the sermon. In other words, the pastor couldn't have been aiming the sermon at Al. But God had.

By now, Al had shifted to his stubborn mode. He was not in a good mood—Christmas was coming up and he was going to be by himself in Knoxville. And, he was aggravated because after the fiasco of the first step, his counselor had told him he was not on the "28-day plan."

Ignoring Al, the counselors listened to the tape that night (probably, Al says, to make sure that it couldn't be played in reverse to discover a recipe for making drugs) and then handed it to Al.

Alone, he turned the CD on and started listening to Dennis, his pastor. "'You may not be where you want to be this Christmas,'" Dennis began. Al thought, "You've got that right, pastor," but he kept listening. "'You may be thinking that this is going to be the worst Christmas ever, but my Christmas wish for you is that you will have a spiritual awakening and find God's will for you.'" The words hit Al like a water-filled balloon being splashed in his face. "I'm done," he thought.

The next morning, Al was ready to do the first step. "God spoke to me. I knew I was finished," Al confesses, telling God, "Whatever you want me to do, I'll do." And this time he meant it.

It wasn't all downhill, even after he changed his attitude and turned in the right direction. One day he was sitting outside, trying to do the fifth step, and his head sank lower and lower. A pastor, also a recovering alcoholic, came and sat beside him. Listening to the man of God who had been where he had been, Al's heart opened to the words the man spoke: "God will forgive you if you will ask him. Why are you carrying it all around?"

Al says with a smile so radiant it could only come through grace, "It was simple. I fell on my knees."

After 28 days of treatment, Al's counselor said frankly but with compassion, "You're not ready for the world, and the world is not ready for you." So Al entered a half-way house. It wasn't all smooth sledding there, because some days Al had the same attitude he had when he started at Cornerstone. Shedding his ego wasn't easy. One day, he thought he had a better way to do something at the half-way house. His counselor shot him down when he began, "You know, I was thinking...."

"Stop. STOP!" the counselor exclaimed. "Your brain is so addled you probably have two neurons firing, and they accidentally bumped into one another and you thought you had an idea. You didn't. I'll let you know when you can think."

At the half-way house, despite his occasional bad attitude, Al was welcomed by his two roommates, Chris and Flip, who had been there for a while. Flip was a funny character and kept everyone laughing. After a couple of months rooming with Al, Flip was sent back into the world. Sadly, within nine days he had drunk himself to death. Flip's relapse and death opened Al's eyes to the dangers he would face when he returned to the "real" world. Today, he says he has learned the difference in relapse and staying in recovery: "In the Big Book, we are given a daily reprieve contingent upon the maintenance of our spiritual condition."

Since 2005, when Al completed his treatment, he has gone to an AA meeting virtually every day. More importantly, he says, "I hit my knees every morning and every night." For the first few years, he saw a counselor weekly. Once, his counselor told him he thought he was doing well enough to make it on his own. When Al told Liz this, she said, "No way, big boy," and picked up the phone and called the counselor. Al has graduated to once every two weeks now, but he still values the support he receives and plans to continue.

Al is thankful Liz stood by him, knowing she could have bailed, especially since her father died an alcoholic. It was hard to rebuild trust, and Al says, "The only thing that restores trust is the calendar." Fortunately, his kids just accepted his alcoholism and drug addiction as a way of life—it was the only way they had ever known him. He was always there for them, and in some ways, Al says his older son glossed over the problems he was seeing. His younger son was surprised when he found his dad was going for treatment: Do you really have a problem? Is it that bad? Both kids have been supportive.

Forgiving himself was harder than getting family support. Al remembers that after one of the family sessions at Cornerstone, Liz left mad and Al was angry at himself. Once again, he sat on a bench in front of the facility, his head drooping. Another recovering addict (he called himself RIP—Recovery in Progress) sat down beside Al. "'You made a mistake,'" Rip admonished Al, "'but you aren't a mistake because God made you and God don't make mistakes.'" With this age-old statement, Rip helped Al accept that God had created him with goodness, and that despite all he had done, God still loved him.

Suddenly Al understood.

His first drink in the sixth grade; an alcoholic by the time he graduated from high school; a drug addict in college and on the job—more than three decades dangling from the hook. But he wasn't hopeless. God's grace brought him to sobriety, and today he not only has his pharmacy license restored, he added a nuclear pharmacy endorsement to his credential and now works in the nuclear industry.

Unhooked and hopeful—and as long as he stays on his knees, Al knows he will stay that way.

CHAPTER 19

THE IMPACT OF
SPIRITUALITY ON RECOVERY

Diseases can be our spiritual flat tires—disruptions in our lives that seem to be disasters at the time but end by redirecting our lives in a meaningful way.

THOMAS JEFFERSON

Regardless of religious preference, the larger notion of spirituality is a pervasive topic across the literature of addiction. Half of the twelve steps advocated by NA/AA embrace God or a higher power as the source of recovery. Indeed, many recovering addicts declare their continued sobriety would not be possible without God. Thus, while many definitions of spirituality allow for the exclusion of God, for the purpose of this book, spirituality will be defined as a sense of transcendence that includes the existence of a deity or higher power. For Christians, that higher power is God.

Monteleone has found that believing in a higher power helps a person work through issues. "Without such faith, addicts have no basis for growth. Belief in a higher power helps addicts identify that they have personal value and a purpose for being here." Moreover, Monteleone knows acceptance of a higher power helps connect the addict to humanity in a bigger picture. And, it drives a person's belief system. Monteleone recalls one man who, by his mid-50s, had been through treatment several times. Physically imposing at over 6 feet tall, he was addicted to polysubstances (defined as anything and everything). Monteleone remembers that, in counseling sessions, the man showed little energy and his emotional demeanor was flat. Somberly, Monteleone concedes that, although no addict is ever hopeless, this man came close. "He had no spiritual understanding at all, and he seemed empty of emotion," she notes. Then one day, a peer approached Monteleone and said she needed to talk to the man. Afraid something was wrong, Monteleone went immediately and was shocked to find the man had a big smile on his face. He shared with Monteleone that a fellow patient had led him to God—he had experienced a spiritual conversion. At last, God was real to him. With that underpinning, he went from almost hopeless to absolutely hopeful.

Al confesses he, too, didn't always have hope. "I had gotten to the point death didn't look so bad and life didn't look so good. I kept going and going because I had a family who loved me and a belief in God, even if it wasn't a relationship at that time. My lack of real faith left me with a lack of hope. Most days I had no faith in myself or anybody or anything, but I had a little spark of grace that I hung onto."

In Mark 9:24, a father seeking help for his son cried out, "I believe. Help thou my unbelief." He believed in God, but he knew he still had disbelief in his heart—an uncertainty that may sometimes be inevitable in the quest for the transcendent part of life. As much as we want to be certain, sometimes the invisibility of it all—the lack of concrete, physical attributes—leaves us groping for faith and conviction.

If spirituality is mysterious and elusive, why would addicts turn to it for hope? Perhaps because at the bottom of the pit, no other hope remains. Or, perhaps because in the indefinable part of the spirit called "soul," the message of hope was written in indelible ink long before physical birth. And, does it really matter why? If an addict has admitted he is powerless over his disease, and his belief in a higher power brings a lifeline to recovery, does he have to understand its complexities?

How can the addict tap this intangible source of help? In *Life's Healing Choices*, Baker lists three beliefs as requisite to connecting to an unseen power:

- Believe that God exists.
- Believe that you matter to Him.
- Believe that He has the power to help.

The belief part, as the father in Mark's gospel found, can come and go; it can be certain or tenuous, but we only have to turn to the reservoir of nature for definitive proof. From the synchronization of the moon and the tides, to the magical way a man and woman's body fit together to form new life, to the cycles of rebirth in nature, evidence abounds that a master plan was designed and is in operation. While we may not be able to explain how it all started—where God came from—we can see enough to know without question that His hand is in our world.

If God's hand created the world—and all that is in it, including humans—then surely we matter to Him. And, if He had the wisdom and command to fling the moon and stars into place and divide the waters with land, we should have no doubt He has the power to help addicts recover. Terry C claimed that power and speaks with confidence about his trust in God. When he let go of his powerlessness, he let go forever. While he knows he was responsible for cleaning his own house and for controlling the parts he can control, he does not hesitate to ask for help from his higher power when he needs it.

INNER JOURNEY

Addiction not only affects thought processes, it also masks the inner being—the place where you are you. In *Hamlet*, Shakespeare wrote, "This above all: to thine own self be true/and it must follow, as the night the day/Thou canst not be false to any man." Under the influence of alcohol or drugs, a person's internal compass gets disabled. Acting out of character, the addict wonders, "Who am I?" Loss of identity—the loss of the self she believed she was—is disorienting. "If I am not who I was, am I who I have become?" When the person she has become is not someone she is proud to be, her self-confidence shrinks and her spirit spirals downward.

Sylvia knows what it is like to become someone she didn't want to be—someone whose value system was alien to her even though it had directed her life for years. Under the long-term influence of drugs, Sylvia's spirit became barren; she felt restless, knowing she had lost her sense of direction—no longer guided by her lifelong beliefs. Amazingly, after only days of sobriety, she remembers thinking, "I am me again." With an unaltered mind, she knew who she had been and who she was becoming again. For the first time in more than a decade, her outer self and her inner self existed in harmony.

MEANING AND PURPOSE

Even under the influence of alcohol or drugs, the soul can yearn—spiritual hunger can drive the addict to seek relief. An innate sense of something more and better refuses to die.

It was that sense of a purpose beyond himself that allowed Victor Frankl to survive the horrors of the Auschwitz concentration camp. As he watched friends and family die daily in the human ovens, he despaired. Eventually, he discovered that prisoners who lost faith in their future doomed themselves because they dropped their spiritual hold, followed by mental and physical decay. In his book, *Man's Search for Meaning*,

Frankl reminds his readers of Nietzsche's words, "He who has a why to live for can bear with almost any how." With an aim or purpose, prisoners could rise above the horrific "how" of their existence.

Frankl surmised that what was needed was a fundamental change in the prisoners' attitude toward life—that he needed to teach the despondent, hopeless men that "it did not really matter what we expected from life, but rather what life expected from us." Instead of focusing on the nebulous meaning of life, prisoners had to respond in concrete ways to their destiny. If a man's destiny was to suffer, that became his task and purpose. And, Frankl, again quoting Nietzsche, told fellow prisoners, "That which does not kill me, makes me stronger." The meaning of life, according to Frankl, includes "suffering and dying, deprivation and death." The hopelessness of the struggle, Frankl averred, did not detract from its dignity and its meaning. His thirst for life was greater than his fear of death, and he made an inner decision to decide that only he could control his mind and his spirituality. He refused to let depravity of the Nazis defeat his spirit and his desire to find meaning even through suffering.

If prisoners of concentration camps can find meaning in the midst of depressing degradation and terrifying torture, then surely we can rise above our problems, which pale by comparison. Surely we can search for a purpose permeated with meaning and hopeful of fulfilled goals.

Without a mind altered by chemical substances, reflection and self-examination can restore the moorings of soul and spirit. The meaning of life itself—and an addict's individual life—can be unlocked. Nietzsche's well-known lines undergird the motivation for many addicts to recover: If an addict has family or friends to live for, she has the "why" to bear the "how" of withdrawal and sobriety. Although Sherry feared many times Sylvia would take her own life in the depths of her despair, Sylvia says it was never an option. Her children—and grandchildren—stayed firm, even in the midst of her altered mind, as the "why" of her existence.

Robert Byrne wrote, "The purpose of life is a life of purpose." Simple yet confusing. At the heart of life is a yearning for peace. We live, in Thoreau's words, "lives of quiet desperation." This is especially true of those addicted. Desperate to change but desperate for drugs or alcohol. When the desperation for change becomes stronger than the desperation for another pill or drink, the addict has found the will to live—the will to find meaning and peace in life.

OPENNESS

As Matthew 12:25 states, a house divided against itself cannot stand.

In the same sense, a person divided against himself will fall. An addict whose life is divided by drug or alcohol abuse—one part fighting against continued use and another wielding the weapon of "gotta have it"—will eventually cave in. The embattled life inevitably becomes insular and closed, avoiding openness that would allow others to challenge the destructive habits.

An old Ethiopian folk truism states, "When spider webs unite, they can tie up a lion." The webs an addict weaves tie him up in the same way—webs of lies and deceptions make a labyrinth from which it is difficult to escape. Often it takes a broomstick of disaster to pull the web down. At other times, opening oneself to others offering assistance will disintegrate the web, allowing the addict to reconnect to the world.

CONNECTEDNESS

Connections to the world may come through family or friends, or they may be found in support groups, including AA/NA, Celebrate Recovery, and religious organizations. Splintered families can heal, although it takes time; and if they don't, the recovering addict can find other connections to fill the void.

As Conger (1994) noted, all of us are connected to one another and to the world beyond ourselves. He adds that "Spirituality, more powerfully than most other human forces, lifts us beyond ourselves and our narrow self-interests." For the addict, this means connecting first to self—the reuniting of mind, body, and spirit—and then expanding the reach to others. Only then can true purpose and meaning in life be rediscovered.

BEYOND SPIRITUALITY CONCEPTS

For the more than 75 percent of Americans who are Christians, spirituality goes beyond concepts of the inner being, purpose and meaning, openness, and connectedness. It is an intensely personal, one-on-one experience with their God and with fellow Christians. They believe, as Isaiah 43:2 states, that God will be with them when they go through deep waters and great trouble. They know that they may go through rivers of difficulty, but they also know they will not drown. Even if they walk through the fires of life, they will not be consumed.

Tapping this saving power requires that Christians—and many people of other devout religions—believe God's power is accessible whenever they ask. All that is required is to believe and turn the powerlessness of their lives over to the all-powerful being by whatever name they call him.

Pulling free of the abuse hook is not easy, especially if the addict's life is in sinking sand. But a cry for help from the spirit—even when the human voice cannot utter the words—is heard. The answer may come in many forms, and it is not necessarily instantaneous, but it always comes. As the old song goes, "In His time, He make all things beautiful." He can take the life destroyed by abuse and make it lovely and whole again. All the addict has to do is cry out to Him for help.

On the worst night of Sylvia's addiction, as she lay on her bed in shame and humiliation, she sobbed until she could cry no more and then fell asleep. That night a dream changed her life.

Sylvia

My dream was so real I will never doubt God again. For the past few months, I had been having the same dream every night. I would dream I was driving down the road toward my old childhood home in Chattanooga Valley. In every dream the road would get so dark I couldn't see where I was going. Panicked, I knew I was about to wreck. And I did—every dream would end with my crashing just before I woke up trembling.

I had the same dream the night of my last arrest, but the end was different. In the blackness of night, unable to see, this time I was running instead of driving down the same road. I could hear cars coming toward me, but the road was so dark I didn't know which way to go. Suddenly, an intensely bright light appeared to my right. As I turned toward the light, I started seeing more and more lights moving toward a huge, brighter illumination in the sky. As I started running toward the radiating lights, my mother, who died 26 years ago, appeared and with her arms around me, we began running toward the lights in the sky together. All the lights were moving toward a huge mass of lights in the sky and for an instant I saw a figure in the middle of the lights. I knew I was seeing God, and I started screaming, "Oh, my God, Oh, my God." I woke myself up screaming and immediately I knew God had given me that dream. I knew exactly what it meant. I had been going down that dark road for so long, headed toward disaster without any hope because God wasn't in my life. But after surrendering my addiction to him, God was showing me I was finally on the right road, and he was guiding me by His light.

I have no doubt whatsoever that the dream was a message from God. I woke up the next morning and was happier and more peaceful than I had been in 17 years, even though I still faced daunting legal problems. It was amazing what having God back in my life did for me.

I've been pill free for almost two years and although I don't have a home or money, or any of the worldly possessions I once treasured, I'm still joyful. I have no desire for pills and know as long as I stay close to God and live for him I never will.

I turned my addiction over to God, but more importantly, I surrendered my life, my problems, my family, and my future to Him. I lived with problems I couldn't deal with for more than 20 years. Some of those same problems still exist, but after I decided to stop using, nothing could have made me take the bait that would only have given me a temporary escape. I just wish it hadn't taken me so long to realize that God can do for us what we can't do for ourselves. My life could have been so different. He was there waiting for me to give up my addiction and turn my messed up life over to him. All I had to do was to be willing, and He would do the rest.

That's the kind of difference God can make in the life of any addict. It is where spirituality begins.

CHAPTER 20

UNHOOKED AND HOPEFUL:

David and Ronelle S's Personal Story

Part 1 - David

four years sober and free of drugs, David knows his addiction odyssey was a manifestation of what was happening inside him. At an early age, perhaps to rebel against his military father's authoritarian control and his ironclad approach to the Christian life, David found it exhilarating to do anything he knew was wrong. At eight years old, he and a cousin finished off cigarette butts they scavenged in the yard. At 12, he smoked marijuana on the back of the school bus. Although he smoked a few more joints over the next few years, alcohol became his substance of choice.

David likely inherited his vulnerability to alcohol from his dad, who had given up drinking before David was born. He describes his dad as a "dry drunk," meaning he no longer drinks but has never dealt with the problems that fueled his addiction. A Naval officer in charge of security at a base in Bermuda, his father carried a bag full of resentment wherever he went. On one side an egotistical man who believed he walked on water; on the other side a man who didn't think very highly of himself. It was a love-hate relationship waging an ongoing war within the man's mind, taking its toll not only on the naval officer but also on his son.

Hanging around the military base in Bermuda, David soon thought drinking at all hours of the day and night was normal. And occasionally, shoplifting was an exciting way to spend an afternoon. Even when his mother took him to a juvenile home, trying to scare him, it didn't work.

Later, he worked on base as part of the grass crew, where dope and alcohol were part of a day's work. Unbeknownst to David, one day he got hold of some high potency stuff. He wound up getting so high he drove a riding lawn mower across the naval base runway before cutting crop circles on the baseball field. But David's dad ranked high on the totem pole, and no one wanted to get on his bad side by telling him his kid had been high, so they just transferred him to the PX, where he promptly started stealing clothes.

David's dad suspected his son sometimes violated his strict code but couldn't prove it until David was spied hiding three joints in the back yard, and his dad demanded the marijuana. The stalwart Christian father lied to the base officers, telling them David had found the joints. Another lesson learned: It's okay to lie to avoid getting in trouble. In truth, David's dad probably wasn't as concerned about consequences for David as he was about his own image.

But it wasn't over. After the officers left, David's dad took him to his room, cursing him, and hit him forcefully in the face. To avoid future incidents that might look bad on him, David's father sent him to Charleston, S.C., to live with his grandmother. It didn't work out and upon returning to Bermuda, David ran away—the third time since he was twelve. His father took him back to the airport, gave him $75 from his savings account and grumbled, "All I can say to you, is best to you, son."

David could have cared less. Free from his parents, he hustled, conned, stole—and partied. He admits he went through some regrettable relationships with women, including an older Japanese woman, and a brief, failed marriage. When drinking and partying grew old, David decided to join the Army, so he could turn his life around. Instead, he got busted in rank twice—once for insubordination and once for failure to show up for PT. Although he went through an addiction treatment program in the army, David didn't have a clue he had a problem. The culture he lived in seemed normal to him—he had only three concerns: drugs, alcohol, and women. Looking back, David says, "I didn't think rationally. I just had a good time." In the midst of the fun times, he left his wife.

After an honorable discharge from the Army, David had nothing— no car, no high school diploma, no home. For seven years he partied. He remembers those years with nostalgia: "I felt so free. I didn't have any of life's burdens—no job, no wife, no responsibility. I was totally unencumbered and I loved it." Cocaine became his pleasure. He recalls thinking, "I wish I had an IV drip with cocaine 24 hours a day." But one day his heart felt fluttery after doing too much cocaine, and David knew something wasn't right. Frightened he might be dying, like a bolt of lightning, he realized, "If I die here, I want to go to heaven." Humbled, he asked Christ to come into his heart.

Initially, David says, a change occurred, but it was uneven. He vacillated between drunkenness and sobriety, totally relapsing within six months. It was never the same, though. Before his encounter with God, he was carefree about his addiction. "I could do whatever I wanted without guilt." Afterward, when he lost the struggle to stay sober, he felt an overwhelming sense of shame—God trying to rein him in, David believes.

After training to be an EMT and becoming disillusioned with that avenue as a career, David worked as a security guard at a local shopping mall while attending college with the goal of becoming a Physician's Assistant. There he crossed paths with the assistant marketing director, Ronelle, and quickly became enamored with her.

With a grin, he asks, "Can you imagine a girl taking me home to meet parents who were pillars of the Baptist church? Their daughter presents this guy with no driver's license because of multiple DUIs and no high school diploma. David adds, tongue-in-cheek, "Ronelle's biggest problem in life was having one cavity." Valedictorian of her high school class, college cheerleader who graduated magna cum laude, and on and on—the "perfect" daughter. By comparison, she was bringing in a delinquent, David thought to himself. It wasn't that he didn't have ambition. But he had so much baggage, it was hard to get from where he was to where he wanted to be. Over her parents' objections, Ronelle married David.

David confesses he was oblivious to what his addiction was doing to his wife and his marriage for the first 12 years. He imbibed sporadically while completing a college degree, managing to drink and remain functional. "I was a binge alcoholic, the worst kind to help, because everyone around you including yourself says you can't be an alcoholic because you don't drink every day. I knew part of my effort to completely make the change was Ronelle—she was stable; she wasn't a quitter. She often confronted me. I understood God wanted me to be committed to her."

Ronelle's efforts to keep David on a straight and narrow path created resentment, often taking David back to some place where he perceived a loss of power. David concedes he will do anything to get back power when he feels someone has taken it away.

Despite struggling with drinking, David finished college and was accepted into a highly regarded Physician's Assistant school at Wake Forest. His stay there was short. Perhaps it was growing up in the military, but David was a nomad. Constantly picking up his tent and moving.

After leaving Wake Forest, David and Ronelle returned to Chattanooga, where David worked at a local convention center but continued his occasional binge drinking. A year later, he got his dream job— pharmaceutical rep, a job that paid well and one of which he could be proud. But, like his dad, David was two people. On one side was the reprobate and bum—the liar, thief, and lawbreaker. On the other side was a man who desperately wanted to do right.

Along with the other benefits of being a pharmaceutical rep, the job required taking physicians out to dinner, where drinks flowed freely. Justifying drinking became easy. It wasn't long before David ventured down the cocaine chasm and couldn't stop sliding. "It became absolutely impossible for me to function. Toward the end, I couldn't put two days together. I wanted to get high all the time. I had absolutely no control over it."

After a company dinner where he had been drinking, David downed a couple of Xanax. His eyes so blurry he couldn't tell where the road was, David's weaving car was stopped by an angel of mercy. When he told the cop he was a pharmaceutical rep, the officer was sympathetic, saying he didn't want to ruin his life. So he let David call Ronelle to come get him. When she called her father to go with her so she could drive David home, the secret she had held inside for 12 years could no longer remain hidden.

The next day, David stayed home, alleging illness, but in truth, he needed more pills and liquor. Later in the day, tearing out of the house when Ronelle refused to buy more beer, David demolished a mailbox on their street. Although a neighbor summoned police, David was let off easily—two tickets—one for failing to stay in his lane and one for not reporting an accident. Unscathed, he paid a $35 ticket and went scot-free. Twice in 24 hours he had gotten off with no more than a slap on the wrist when he should have gone to jail. But it was a close call: Fifteen minutes after he hit the mailbox, a school bus would have been letting students off at that spot. He shudders today just thinking about it.

Some time later, just before he was to meet Ronelle in Tybee Island, Ga., where she was on a business trip, David admits he got so high he couldn't walk. Fearing he had overdosed, David cried out for help to his father-in-law. That night, Ronelle's parents heard for the first time that David was using cocaine. It had been bad enough when they had learned he was a binge alcoholic the night he was stopped by the police—

adding drugs to the picture was devastating. The worst part was that their daughter had fought her demons alone for 12 years, telling no one. Amazingly, Ronelle's father listened and then said, "We'll get through this."

For years, David had blamed his problems on someone else. Money wasn't a big issue since he and Ronelle both had good jobs, although she did begin to notice large chunks of money disappearing at the end. But David was a virtuoso liar, and Ronelle was naturally naïve, so for a long time he managed to assure her the money had gone for legitimate purposes.

His father-in-law wasn't as gullible as Ronelle and knew David must have treatment. Realizing he would lose his support if he didn't seek help, David agreed to go to a North Carolina treatment center. After a long drive through the mountains, David balked at going in because the place reminded him of bitter times with his father. With Ronelle sobbing, the whole family trekked back home. But it wasn't over. The next day his father-in-law took David to a local treatment center where David threatened suicide to get admitted, using buzz words that pushed him to the head of the admissions list.

It took three attempts at treatment before, in David's words, "I finally bought into the program hook, line, and sinker. I knew there was no chance I was going back into drugs and alcohol."

Two months later, David came home, scared to death. The first night he broke down and cried in the shower. Without his safety net, petrified he couldn't make it, David's resolve to quit drove him to attend AA meetings every day for a year and then joined a church group called Celebrate Recovery.

Through treatment and follow-up care, David learned accountability— responsibility for his actions— and that he must be careful because he has a predisposition for alcohol and drugs. "Once I drink," he says, "my brain goes haywire."

Sobriety not only restored rational thinking but also gave David his voice back. As an eight-year-old, one of his teachers had made fun of a joke he told. That was the day he stopped speaking in public. "I never thought I would stand in front of people and talk," but he now teaches Sunday School. God did that, David says. "God brought me where I needed to be. He keeps me sober—following Him and enlisting the help of others helps me maintain sobriety on a daily basis."

David had more good fortune than many addicts. Although he had DUIs, stole, and committed other illegal acts, his record is clear. He should have gone to prison, but it never happened. Like the "King Baby," David felt he was king of his own world and that when he finally made a turn to do what he was supposed to do, he would be successful, almost effortlessly. But, following the pattern of the king baby, he found he didn't have all the pieces. Even when he met Ronelle, thinking he had made the final turn, he had not faced all of his issues and problems, and she couldn't save him, as hard as she tried. That took a higher power.

Part 2 – Ronelle

Ronelle and David had polar opposite childhoods. While he was getting a thrill doing anything he knew he shouldn't, Ronelle spent her days pleasing her parents. An only child, she grew up with limitless love and attention, and she made her doting parents proud. Smart, outgoing, and popular, she sailed through high school and college working hard, making friends, and enjoying her sheltered life.

Because he was the first male since junior high to ask Ronelle to go to church with him, David made quite an impression. Ronelle thought she had found the perfect mate—handsome, charming, and a real Christian. Together they studied scripture, prayed, and fell in love.

David was honest with Ronelle about his previous marriage and even told her he had experimented with drugs, had drunk some, and had partied a lot, but it was all in the past—and the sanitized version of his life didn't sound too bad to someone who had never been around this lifestyle. Plus, she remembers thinking she could show David how different life could be with someone who loved him, encouraged him, and wanted the best for him. (What she didn't know was she was the one who would have to face a "different" life—at least for the first decade of her marriage.) Her parents, who knew about David's previous marriage and his prior DUIs, weren't quite as hopeful about their future son-in-law. Her father told her, "If you marry him, you're going to have consequences the rest of your life." Today, Ronelle yields, "My dad is always right." In retrospect, Ronelle wonders how she could have been so blind.

It took only a few weeks of marriage for Ronelle to realize something was wrong. David didn't come home one night after work. Sometime after midnight he called, and she could hear background noise. When she asked when he was coming home, he replied, "When I want to."

"I felt like he had been drinking," Ronelle recalls. When David showed up at 3 a.m., she locked him out of their bedroom, scared because she had never been around a drunk. The next day, he told her she better not ever do that again. She didn't know what he meant, and she didn't want to find out. Strangely, as close as she was to her parents, she didn't call them.

David's drinking took on a pattern—at first he would get drunk every four to six months or so. Ronelle began to fear any occasion that might be a cause for him to take a drink—her birthday, his birthday, their anniversary, a holiday, anything could be the reason. Anytime he took one drink, Ronelle says, "I would get sick inside. I knew why: He would say I'm only going to have one beer to celebrate, but he couldn't stop."

David was a master manipulator. For the first eight or nine years instead of apologizing to Ronelle after one of his binges, he argued, "If I could just down three or four drinks whenever I wanted, I wouldn't have to cram it all in when I got a chance." In other words, "It's all your fault because you hassle me."

Although part of their marriage was good, after four years Ronelle felt she was leading a double life. She held the dirty truth inside, dying a little every time David got drunk. She couldn't bring herself to tell anyone, especially her parents. And David played on her reluctance, saying, "What are you going to tell your parents if you leave me? Are you going to tell them I had three or four beers too many?" David was well aware of the idealized picture Ronelle's parents held of their daughter and used that as a weapon to keep her silent.

For her part, Ronelle says, "I couldn't let my parents know I had screwed up the biggest decision in my life. It was hard for me to even admit that to myself." Once at an aerobics class, she started crying. "I so wanted to tell my friend who was there that day, but I didn't want her to know how bad things were. I didn't want her to think poorly of David." One day another friend came to visit, and Ronelle broached the subject, but she didn't say much. She felt some safety because the friend was going away and wouldn't be around. But the worst of it—how much David was drinking and how bad their relationship was—she held back. She had enough on her hands, dealing with David's erratic job patterns—including getting into a coveted PA program only to leave weeks later, despite her changing jobs to move to another state with him.

A year later, their marriage on smoother ground, they decided to have a baby. A couple of months after their daughter was born, the drinking picked up again. Then, for a couple of years, David seemed to get better. That ended when David started the pharmaceutical job. Soon, David's cycle of binge drinking was every seven days. When he was stopped by the police officer after drinks and a couple of Xanax, the sordid saga of his life could no longer be hidden from her parents. Twelve long years she had held her dark secret inside. Twelve years she had suffered and endured alone. On the way home with David, when he discovered her dad had brought her and thus knew he was drunk, he went ballistic, crazy mad. "It was the first time I was really, really scared."

The next day, Ronelle decided to go to her Mom and Dad's. "I couldn't handle my life alone anymore." Her life was so bad even the embarrassment of everyone knowing wasn't enough to keep her with David. But she didn't get out of the house fast enough. David wanted her to go get him some beer. When she refused, he said he would go himself. Premonition panicking her, Ronelle begged him not to go. Minutes later, David came back in the door, all bloody.

When the crisis of the mailbox incident had calmed, Ronelle packed a few clothes and toys in a bag and left. Not sure what he might do, she took the keys to both of the couple's vehicles and David's gun. "At that point, I didn't admit to myself that I was done, but I was pretty close to that." Within days, David was pitiful, horrified at what he had done. Scared of what he said he would do without her, Ronelle returned home.

A few weeks later, for the first time David did not return home all night. Fearing he was dead or in jail and sick of never knowing what was going to happen next, Ronelle packed up and went to her parents' house—she was finally done with him. Soon, a pastor at their church called and told her David was with him. "You need to come talk with him."

"I don't think so," Ronelle responded courageously from her weary soul. But the pastor was insistent, and like a lamb, Ronelle followed the shepherd. At the pastor's office, she was told David wanted to change.

"I mean no disrespect, but I have heard this before," Ronelle declared, standing her ground. But again, the pastor was insistent, saying everyone should pray over Labor Day and then decide what to do.

"Again, I mean no disrespect, pastor, but by Tuesday, the cycle will have started again. If we don't do something right now, our window will have passed."

"I had always believed in the power of prayer," Ronelle admits, "but for the first time I felt prayer would not be enough. David needed help. Someone who could help him face his demons. What they didn't tell me that day—something David would admit a year later—he was on cocaine."

Heeding the directive of her pastor, Ronelle went home with David. As she predicted, by Tuesday, David said he didn't need help. He would be fine.

From a seven-day drinking cycle, David escalated to every three to four days. Burdened, at the end of her rope, Ronelle talked to another person on her church's staff. He gave her a number—his sister's—to call. "You will find she can relate to what's happening to you."

The next time David got drunk, Ronelle called. The voice on the other end of the phone was like the soothing sound of a harp: "The first thing I want you to know is that you are not crazy. What has happened to you happened to me, and it has happened to others."

Hearing that what she was feeling was normal sounded lyrical; angels singing in her head for the first time in years. The lady recommended a book called *Boundaries*. Ronelle purchased it but didn't open it for a week. When she finally got the courage to begin reading, she looked at one page, and crying, shut the book. "It was so painful that I couldn't stand seeing my life in print." After she went back to the book, Ronelle lamented, "If I had just read this book 10 years ago; if I had just told one person what my life was, how different my life might have been."

After the accidents, it was a long eight or nine months before David talked seriously about going into rehab. Finally arrangements had been made for David to enter treatment on March 17. March 18 was a big day for Ronelle; she was mistress of ceremonies for an awards ceremony at the convention center in town and was thankful David would be safely in treatment when the big day arrived. When David's admission was delayed until March 18, Ronelle was frantic. Who knew what David would do in the next 48 hours? What happened was worse than anything she could have imagined. When David arrived home around 1 a.m., what he told her knocked her into a nosedive: He confessed he had been doing cocaine.

Devastated, Ronelle didn't sleep all night. She didn't know if she could pull herself together for the awards event, but she did, taking herself to that hidden place behind the smile. As usual, David had tried to make her feel guilty about going to a work event. Work and aerobics had been Ronelle's escape for years. It was the only time she could focus on something with her whole mind. "Even when I was praying," she confides, "I was smack dab in the middle of David's problems."

It was an unbroken cycle. When they arrived at the treatment center, and he announced he wasn't going in, Ronelle dropped to the floor and wept. Heartbroken, all hope gone.

"The only way I had made it through the last month was that I knew he was going to get help. 'If I could just hold on that long', I had thought, 'God and the counselors would take it from there.' Now we were taking him back with us. Nothing had changed."

Over the years, Ronelle had convinced herself, "If I could clean better (David is a neat freak), if I could look better, if I could...he would love me enough to want to quit the drug use and drinking. I blamed myself. If I could just not care if he drank one or two, he would be okay. He was the master manipulator at putting me in a tailspin, making me think I was crazy, that nothing was really wrong. Over and over he told me as long as he was trying, I had to stay with him—that I needed to give him unconditional love. Those were the things that drove me insane and kept me from leaving or getting help."

Church had always been Ronelle's safe place, and David tried to pry her away from her refuge. If she went alone, a major fight ensued. If she made him go, a battle of epic proportions occurred as they drove to church. "What had been my sanctuary became the worst possible place on earth. When we did make it to church, it seemed everything was aimed at getting David's attention; but when we got into the car and I asked him what he thought, he just tore the sermon or music apart. Crushed, I would sink into my seat and try to hold the sobs back."

For Ronelle, the final straw came while she was in Tybee Island, Ga. She had tried to book a one-way flight, because David, their daughter Savannah, and her parents were planning to drive there, pick her up, and then head to Florida for vacation. When David dropped her off at the airport, she had a sick feeling that something wasn't quite right. For months, this always happened in advance of one of David's binges. It was like she knew when he was going to take that first drink and not be able to stop.

"I tried to convince myself it would be okay, but just before we touched down in the city near Tybee Island, I had the same feeling. As soon as I deplaned, I tried to call David, but he didn't answer. I quickly called our bank and found he had withdrawn $600. It wasn't unusual for $300-400 to disappear on a daily basis, but David easily explained it away each time. When I finally talked to David a few hours later, he told me, 'If you must know, I bought you a birthday present.' Although her birthday was only days away, Ronelle didn't buy the story: "David, that's a lie, and I can't take any more of your lies. Mom and Dad will come on to Florida, but you stay home. I'm done.'"

Taken aback, David asked, "What do you mean?" but Ronelle hung up and called her mother.

"Mom, do you have Savannah?"

"Yes, she's right here."

"Mom, you need to protect my child. I don't know what's going to happen. This is going to end. David has been spending money. I think he is doing drugs. Protect my child." She knew David was not in his right mind and had no idea what he would do.

That night was when David almost overdosed and her dad responded to his call for help.

Ronelle says she couldn't have said what her dad did that night, that "We're going to get you through this."

"I was done," she acknowledges. "I can take and take and take until I snap. I knew when my heart and mind got to that point, nothing would make me go back."

The week after David went to treatment, she told her mother, "I can't pray about this anymore. You pray, and if God tells you I should stay with David, then I will. But I can't be the one to listen with an open heart and mind." After 12 years of living in torment, she didn't even know the man she had married. She didn't want him to come home.

That same week Ronelle's mother told her she believed God would not have allowed her painful journey without a plan for David's life. Her mom was her best friend and role model. If she had faith, Ronelle would trust that and cling to it.

When David finished treatment, though, she felt trapped. He had been there two months, had worked through the Twelve Step program and more, and he was back in church. One of the counselors told her it would take a year to make any difference at all and two years for life to get where David would seem normal. "I can't do that," Ronelle recalls thinking.

"But how could I leave? I wished I had gone when he was so bad, but it was too late. I was stuck. Our life was still terrible—bad fights and horrible times I don't even want to think about." Holding to a glimmer of hope was not easy at times and often felt like sheer torture. She had to take it one day at a time, praying and claiming God would take care of the rest.

During this period, their church was looking for a new minister, and Ronelle began praying for a pastor who had a heart for people with addictions. "I will never forget the night the committee presented their recommendation—when they described Robby, a recovering addict, I started sobbing. And, for the first few months, each time I saw our new pastor, I couldn't stop the tears streaming down my face. Robby was a symbol that God had not forgotten me. He had heard my cry and answered beyond what I asked or could have imagined." When her pastor told his own sordid story, suddenly she felt it was all right for people to hear the dreadful life she and David shared. Before that, she found it hard to listen to David tell others about his addiction. "When I heard him, I was mad; I was hurt all over again. I felt stupid. How did I marry him? How did I not see all this?"

A few weeks after the new pastor arrived, David became the leader of Celebrate Recovery, an addiction group he had been instrumental in starting at their church. Today, David teaches Sunday School and Ronelle is back singing in the choir. It means a lot to Ronelle, who grew up in a home where serving in church was expected and enjoyed. "I never thought after all we had been through we could ever be used." Ironically, Ronelle says, "Of all the things God could use...I've always hated alcohol. How is it that I married an alcoholic? How is it that our testimony stems from a barrel full of drugs and liquor? All our dirty laundry now hangs out for everyone to see.

"People saw me as having a perfect life. Always smiling and singing. I think God chose to use me this way because everyone thought I had it all together, but I was a muddy mess. He took that soiled life we had no hope of coming out of and here we are—David is sober and drug-free and has been for four years.

"Today I want others who are struggling to know, I have never been perfect, but my life appeared 'charmed' to others. Telling people about the blackest days of my life is tough, but I do it because it can give others hope. I tell everyone if I can get through all I did, you can get through your situation, too."

Even so, for the first two years after David went into recovery, Ronelle wondered if she would ever again find the man she married. "I didn't," she admits. "I found someone better." She is quick to add, "But that doesn't always make it easy."

Ronelle says she grew up in a bubble. "Nothing bad had ever happened in my life. I grew up thinking if you work hard and make the 'right' decisions, life would be good. I had always accomplished everything I had set out to do. College, the job I wanted, the husband I had prayed for. Then suddenly my 'perfect' life was anything but perfect."

It has taken Ronelle a long time to recover her own sense of self. She spent so much time and energy trying to make everything okay, she almost lost who she was. Walking on eggshells for more than a decade to avoid triggering a drinking episode reshaped her as a silhouette of the person she used to be—in private, her smiles diminished, her effervescent energy stalled. She lost her love for David. With a frankness that only comes from the sanctity of self, Ronelle admits, "At times it appeared David's death might be the best solution for all of us."

Four years out, she rarely even thinks about the possibility of David relapsing. As long as he is reading the Bible, praying, talking to people who keep him accountable, and attending church, she knows it would be hard for David to drink. But she's not as naïve as she once was—she recognizes relapse is always a possibility. "The difference is if he does something now, it's not on me. Before I tried to control the situation, I tried to protect him and myself. Now I choose to make the decision not to worry.

"The day our church voted to call Robby and again on his first day as our pastor, the congregation lifted their voices to sing, 'Great Is Thy Faithfulness.' With tears streaming down my face, the words I had sung many times since childhood suddenly had a completely new meaning. For the first time, I realized had I not gone through the addiction journey with David, I would have missed witnessing God's miracles."

CHAPTER 21

FINDING PEACE IN YOUR LIFE

*Peace does not dwell in outward things, but within the soul; we may pre-
serve it in the midst of the bitterest pain, if our will remains firm and sub-
missive. Peace in this life springs from acquiescence to, not in an exemp-
tion from, suffering.*

FRANCOIS DE FENELON

The lyrics to "Peace in the Midst of the Storm" are alluring, but when
the addict's world collapses at his feet, is it really possible to find peace?
Sobriety is wonderful, freeing the addict from dependence on alcohol
or drugs to deal with his problems, but it does not magically erase the
difficulties that left him battered and windswept, driving him to the first
nibble of the bait. Without the mind-altering substance that helped him
mask his problems, can he be calm and free from anxiety?

Human existence continually produces stressors and setbacks. Troubles
and crises ebb and flow, although not with the rhythm of ocean waves.
Keeping equanimity when the undertow threatens to engulf the
recovering addict takes living from the inside out—facing squalls with a
spirit-filled life.

A LIFELINE TO SAFETY

Parker Palmer tells how, years ago, in the mid-West where whiteouts
could obscure even short distances, far too many people lost their way
to safety and froze to death in a snow bank with their homes only a few
short feet away. To prevent this, prudent farmers and ranchers learned
to tie a rope from the back door to the barn. When they had to feed their
animals, they held on to the lifeline to get from the house to the barn and
back. In the same way, addicts need a lifeline that will keep them on a
safe path when life's gales threaten. That lifeline to sobriety and peace,

even in the strongest storm, is the inner spirit.

On one end of the addict's lifeline is her sobriety. The whiteout (the addiction) is the problem obscuring the way to safety. At the other end of the lifeline, her spirit houses beliefs that offer security even in storms of terrifying proportions.

THE ABC THOUGHT PROCESS

Peace begins when the recovering addict's beliefs are optimistic instead of pessimistic. The farmers and ranchers knew the dangers they faced; they believed they knew how to stay safe, and they knew the consequences they would face if they did not take positive action. Seligman (1990) describes this way of thinking as a matter of ABCs, a model originally proposed by psychotherapist Albert Ellis:

When a person encounters **a**dversity, he reacts by thinking about it. [The rancher sees the approaching blizzard and thinks about his animals in the barn.] His thoughts quickly solidify as **b**eliefs. ["I'll never be able to get to the barn and back in the whiteout. I'll lose my way and freeze to death."] Beliefs, even before they turn into actions, have **c**onsequences because they control how we think. [The rancher is so nervous, he becomes disoriented more quickly than he would if he concentrated on walking a straight path.] The beliefs, positive or negative, are the difference between dejection and hopefulness, between giving up and taking constructive action. The adverse action from the whiteout would be avoidable if the rancher's belief system triggered a constructive response—preparing by tying a lifeline from his back door to the barn. The consequence: the animals could be fed and the rancher could return safely home.

Let's translate the above example into Sylvia's situation at work:

When a person encounters **a**dversity, she reacts by thinking about it. [Sylvia's boss chastises her.] Her thoughts quickly solidify as **b**eliefs. ["I'll never be good enough to please him. It's a waste of time and energy to try."] In addiction, as in all of life's behaviors, beliefs can become so habitual a person doesn't realize they are controlling her thoughts unless she stops and concentrates on them. Sylvia's automatic thought was negative, reinforcing her poor self-image.

Beliefs, even before they turn into actions, have **c**onsequences because they not only control how a person thinks but also how they act. [Sylvia becomes so nervous she makes another mistake, and her boss belittles her again, the consequence.] Her beliefs left her hopeless, unable to take positive action.

Another example of ABCs: Tom, an alcoholic, loses his job. This **a**dversity triggers old **b**eliefs that he has failed again—"I never get a fair shake, so I might as well drink because I'm no good to anyone anyway." The **c**onsequence: a relapse.

What a person believes dictates how he thinks—whether he makes lemonade out of the lemons he has allowed to grow in his life. The first step in turning pessimistic thoughts into optimistic ones is for the addict to be alert to negative thoughts when they try to pull his spirit down. Once he identifies his thoughts as harmful, a person can choose to distract himself by thinking other thoughts, or he can, as Albert Ellis suggested, compare what is happening to him to the worst possible thing that could happen. By comparison, his problem will not seem so bad. If it could always be worse, he can be thankful it is not. This is also called disputing the negative thought—arguing that it is not as catastrophic as it wants to convince the person it is.

In the above example, the **a**dverse action might not be avoidable, but Tom's **b**elief system could refute that he is the problem: "I'm not the only person who got laid off. The economy is bad, and people are losing jobs everywhere. I'll need to get moving fast and work hard to find another job. Who knows? It might be better than the last one." The **c**onsequence: Tom is motivated to seek new employment rather than turning to the lure of a drink to console himself.

LETTING GO OF BITTERNESS

Conquering and overcoming negative thoughts is the first step in finding peace. Requisite to this step is turning away from bitterness. Were "Love your enemy" not a Biblical commandment, it would still be necessary if a person's spirit is to be free to create positive thinking. Part of the addict wants to hang on to the wrongs and hurts. That makes taming of her will tough—but the addict must let go of hostility. If she is having difficulty releasing the air out of anger, it may help to remember Joseph's response to his brothers who sold him into slavery: "You meant evil against me; but God meant it for good" (Genesis 50:20, NKJV). Just as the betrayal of Joseph by his brothers ultimately saved them from starvation, slavery to addiction may someday be used for good if the addict lets go of her bitterness.

Bonnie St. John, author of *Live Your Joy*, avows that each person has the opportunity to live with bitterness or joy. Despite dealing with a leg amputation, years of childhood abuse, divorce, and single motherhood, she chose joy and has found that it comes "from the inside out." Through the challenges life threw in her face, she found joy can still be discovered gradually, like paddling down a flowing river of grace. The journey leads to a belief that well-being can exist through good and bad. This sense of well-being emanates from warm springs of faith, hope, and love, where confidence seasons life.

St. John is not a Pollyanna. She concedes finding joy in the midst of problems is not an easy task, but she is convinced that with authenticity, humility, vision, positivity, friendship, resilience, and faith, joy is out there, just waiting for us to claim it.

Joy should be viewed as a reservoir, St. John says, reminding us that sometimes the reservoir is full and sometimes it is just "plain empty." It takes work, she says, to fill it back up, but she also reminds us that the level can always be raised because joy comes from inside us, not from an outside source. Acknowledging that we won't fly on cloud nine every day, St. John believes we can learn to create joy if we stop being a slave to what is happening in our world. Every person holds the power to become master of his or her own destiny. When we drain bitterness out of the reservoir, it can be filled with joy, and St. John proclaims, then we will not only find greener grass and brighter colors, but also challenges that are less unnerving. In short, a better life.

RENEWED STRENGTH

Without the tart taste of resentment and with the shield of thought control, the recovering spirit is freed to be filled with strength and courage to ride the waves of life. At times in the addict's life, he will still feel hurt and alone, but he can learn to use those experiences as pathways to spiritual growth. When tempted to recapture what was a temporary fix for his problems, it is good to remember that what lies on the other side of the chasm may bring new peace and joy. The journey itself—when the addict copes with whatever life throws his way—can teach him that he has hidden strength. With positive thoughts and determination, he can make it through the toughest valley. Even so, he should not be too hard on himself if he momentarily loses his foothold.

We are all imperfect human beings, and the addict's spirit should not sink when she can't handle stress on any given day. Peace is sometimes as elusive as a butterfly flitting its way in and out of the addict's line of vision as it sips nectar from fragrant flowers. Still, if she holds a steady vigil, if she trusts a higher power to keep her safe when she is in perilous waters, her spirit will grow, and with it, her strength. As Cicero wisely opined, "A man of courage is also full of faith."

Faith gives courage, but human minds drive the daily battle to find peace. Within the letters of the word lies its secret:

Putting away bitterness from life's hurts

Existing with equanimity in the midst of life's problems

Adopting positive beliefs to guide actions

Creating a lifeline to safety

Engaging your spirit for inner strength

Peace can only come from within a person. God makes it freely available, but an addict must accept it as a gift, using his mind and spirit to fight the battle to keep it in his heart when the squalls of life toss him to and fro among the waves.

CHAPTER 22

UNHOOKED AND HOPEFUL:

Robby G's Personal Story

Γobby stands 6 feet, 6 inches tall—a powerful, imposing young man who exudes the peace that comes from within the soul. Even so, if you met him on the street, you wouldn't suspect he is pastor of one of the largest churches in Chattanooga, Tn., any more than you could envision that this handsome guy once sold ecstasy, cocaine, and "Special K" (ketamine). He looks more like a bouncer, a career he once tried for a short time.

But every Sunday he stands in front of more than a thousand, usually in a suit and tie but sometimes dressed more casually, proclaiming the gospel of his risen Lord. It hasn't always been that way, Robby is quick to confess, and he readily tells the story of his once sordid and now spirit-filled life.

"I was not born physically blind, but I was spiritually blind for 26 years," Robby says quietly, almost reverently. Reared in a Catholic home in New Orleans, Robby attended church every Sunday with his family. With a chuckle, he declares, "If we missed, mom had us in confession on Saturday." Despite faithful attendance, Robby admits he never had a relationship with God. God was an authoritative figure—there to keep him in line—not a God of peace. "I saw God as a dictator who was out to spank me when I got off track."

Not overly concerned about religion, Robby's heart and mind were focused on playing basketball at the University of North Carolina Greensboro, where the stand-out high school star had been awarded a full scholarship. When his girlfriend balked about his going so far from home, he gave up his coveted opportunity to play with the Spartans, adding, "I literally opened the phone book and found William Carey College in Hattiesburg,

Mississippi. With a cragged grin, Robby temporarily halts his story to ask with mock derision coloring his words, "Has anyone here ever heard of William Carey College?" Laughter rides a wave across his listeners when only a couple of hands rise into the air.

Knowing nothing about the college, Robby called the coach and asked if he could try out for the team.

"Son, the team starts practice in two weeks; it's a bit late," the coach responded gruffly, ready to hang up until Robby quickly told him about his UNC[G] scholarship. That, combined with his size, convinced the coach to let him walk on. Soon, Robby had a full scholarship at William Carey. It wasn't UNC[G], but he would be on the court, and his girl would be in the stands watching.

When classes started, to his surprise, Robby discovered William Carey was a Southern Baptist school. "Here I was," Robby laments, "a Roman Catholic in a Southern Baptist college. I was the target of every evangelism class on campus. I would drive around in my red Mustang, blaring uncensored rap music. Most of the students were turned off by me. I was the person you never wanted to talk to about Christ."

But one guy was brave enough—Jeremy Brown—probably because he was almost as tall and broad-shouldered as Robby. He shared the gospel with Robby, walked him through a prayer, and Robby concedes, "I confessed my sins—but it didn't last. It was just words." Coming clean, Robby acknowledges he did not experience any change in his life.

Rolling along, having a good time, Robby graduated in 1998 and, with a couple of friends, started a computer business with one goal in mind—make tons of money. The company went well for a while but dissolved eight months later. Cocky and confident, Robby decided he wouldn't work for a while, thinking he could start another business later. For now, training to be a Brazilian Jiu-Jitsu fighter sounded enticing, so that's what he did.

One night a guy in a bar noticed Robby's 6'6" frame—all 285 pounds of it—and asked him if he would work as the head bouncer at his club during Marti Gras. "Do you mean I would get paid to fight?" Robby asked with amusement. "I'm in."

Robby worked at the bar for three months, throwing out the rowdy guys and the ones too drunk to walk. One day, escorting two boisterous men to the parking lot, Robby found his bulk didn't give him the upper hand. Cursing the whole time as he was being shepherded to the parking lot, one of the guys reached under the seat of his car and pulled out a loaded gun. "Now talk to me," the drunk demanded.

Time for a career change. Before that could be accomplished, one night while driving home from work, an 18-wheeler crossed two lanes and rammed Robby's car into a guard rail. Sandwiched between the huge truck and the metal rail, Robby's seat came off its hinges. Lucky to be alive, the ox of a man now had two herniated discs, one bulging in his back.

When he left the hospital, Robby carried home four bottles of prescription pills—Oxycontin, Percocet, Soma, and Valium. "I was 22 years old, had never taken drugs before in my life," he bemoans. "I was legitimately in pain, so I started taking them every 4-6 hours." Within three months, Robby was hooked. A car accident had sent his life spiraling in a new direction—downward.

"I had an insatiable desire to get high," Robby discloses. He met some guys in the city who told him he could actually make money selling drugs— being a user just consumed money; it didn't produce any. And Robby's addiction was expensive. A 30-day supply of prescription drugs ran out in a few days. "I had to find a way to fuel my desire."

With his business background, Robby was easy to convince that dealing drugs was the solution for feeding his addiction—and for making money. It took even less time for him to realize that selling street drugs was even more lucrative. By comparison, fooling around with prescription drugs brought in peanuts.

So Robby took his knowledge from the business world and applied it to the drug world. "Over the next three years, I imported and sold GHB, marijuana, cocaine, heroin, ecstasy, and Special K," he states, adding with a twist, "And the Special K I sold wasn't breakfast cereal."

With stacks of money at his disposal, Robby had it all—a red Mustang Cobra, an apartment in downtown New Orleans, and anything else he desired. "I thought I was indomitable." Yet, deep inside, Robby confesses, "I knew something was missing. There had to be more to life than this."

In the midst of riding high with drugs and money, suddenly a friend died of an overdose with the needle still in his arm. If that wasn't a wake-up call, losing a total of eight close friends—not random acquaintances—to drugs over a three-year-period was an altar call. Six of his buddies went to jail. Clearly, the cops were on to the business Robby reveled in.

The bottom fell out for Robby: "The addiction had overcome me. I couldn't sell drugs fast enough to feed my habit." He went from high rolling to low living—existing in a house with no gas, no heat, no hot water. Then, he admits, "I did the unthinkable. I went to my mom and dad—the mom and dad who had fed me, taken care of me, and loved me." His mind altered by abuse, he stole his dad's credit card from his wallet and memorized the number, charging over $15,000 in a three-month period. Remorsefully, Robby reveals, "I almost bankrupt my family."

That did it. "I'll never forget the phone call from my mother: 'Your dad is furious with you. I am disappointed. Don't ever come to this house again.'"

Smug, Robby brashly told his mom, "You know, I didn't need you anyway."

But three months later he was back knocking on his parents' door. This giant of a man who had never shed a tear, had come home, his face like a mountain stream. "Mom, I can't do it anymore. I need help," he pleaded. Robby's parents sent him to Tijuana, Mexico, for rehabilitation, and for eight months, Robby stayed clean.

After another period of drug use and selling, Robby went back into rehab in November 2002. On the way home, he remembered what Jeremy had told him: "Get down on your knees and pray for God to help you." That's exactly what Robby did. The next day, he told his father he had been called to preach. Teaming with Jeremy, they preached to the homeless, "making magic"—literally. "I didn't know much about preaching, but I had been a magician, so I would do magic tricks before I preached to make people like me." Robby preached all over—from Louisiana to New York. Charismatic and charming, he drew people like birds needing nectar. Robby was living high—on spirit this time, not illegal substances.

Three months later, thinking he had conquered his addiction—that his recovery was unshakable—Robby went back to the drug world to try to save two friends. Regrettably, he found you can't hang with old friends without falling back into the drug culture.

With a pocket full of money from the tractor trailer collision lawsuit, Robby bought a $50,000 Cadillac CTS—a black-on-black beauty with chrome rims, decked out with a $9000 stereo system in the back. In retrospect, Robby knows, "This car triggered the beginning of the downfall of my new life." It was the root of pride, Robby's Achilles' heel. "I went to one of my buddies and boasted, "Look what God is doing in my life. Mind if I talk to you about it?" His buddy responded, "No. Mind if I roll a joint while we talk?" That should have been a powerful message to Robby, but he missed the warning light.

In the process of showing off, Robby was sucked back in.

"Within two weeks, I can't tell you how it happened, or pinpoint when it happened—I was back on drugs." Hooked again. "And this time I had money."

From March to May, Robby spent $28,000 on heroin and cocaine. "I had a $180 a day addiction. Every morning when I woke up I needed $180 to live. I blew the rest partying." With a shake of his head, Robby adds, "The crazy thing was, I was still preaching." He was living two lives, and his mind was so warped by drugs he didn't discern the conflict.

One day, when Robby was trying to lead a young lady to Christ at a bar where he was having his first high-powered drink of the morning, she looked him straight in the eye and said, "For someone who knows so much about Jesus, you sure don't act like it." Today, Robby says, in leading her to Christ, he came back himself. This time, when he went to rehab, God went with him, and his recovery stuck. Within a year he had paid back his parents and was ready to enter seminary. "I still don't know why they let me in," he says with a coy chuckle. And, soon, Robby tacks on, almost with amazement, he will add a doctorate in preaching to his credentials. More importantly to Robby, he is married to the Godliest woman he has ever known and has two precious sons.

As Robby winds down his story, he says he is one of many people within his church who made life-altering mistakes, whose lives were later transformed by their faith.

After sharing his past with his congregation, Robby ended by asking, "Have you ever driven by someone sitting on the side of the road begging?" He holds a cardboard sign that reads, "Homeless. Anything will help."

"I decided to write my story on a piece of cardboard for you to see," Robby discloses as he holds up a sign:

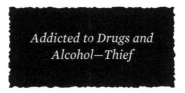

He flips it over and on the back, it reads:

As Robby steps from the stage carrying his cardboard sign, a long line of people walk across the platform at the front of the church, one at a time. Each carries a piece of torn cardboard, much like the one desperate people hold on street corners, asking for food or money. But on each of these pieces of cardboard, there is a confession. As each person takes his turn walking across the stage, he pauses, giving the congregation time to read what he has penciled. Words like "Drug addict," "Stole from my family," and "Drunken husband" tell stories of heartbreak and ruin.

And on and on, more than 30 messages in all. But the messages that bring tears to the eyes of everyone watching the parade of redeemed saints are the words written on the back of the cardboards. After a brief moment, each person turns his sign around. On every piece of ragged cardboard, words of sin and despair change to recovery—hope or joy—on the reverse side.

On and on, the powerful messages of lives transformed by hope and grace stir the emotions of everyone watching and reading the cards.

Sylvia and Sherry sat side by side in this service. Before half of the card bearers had crossed the stage, they turned to each other, eyes brimming with tears. Sherry whispered to Sylvia, choking back sobs, "You should be walking across the stage." After thinking for a moment, Sylvia whispers, "Drugs—I lost who I was for 17 years." I whisper back, "But the other side says, 'Found myself again through God.'"

Like Robby, the first two times Sylvia went through rehab, she did it without a higher power. "Rehab without God is a dead-end street," Robby notes, and Sylvia agrees.

Today, their lost lives regained, Sylvia and Robby are among many who have found that God's grace stands ready at all times, regardless of what a person has done, no matter how low he has fallen. All a person has to do is ask.

Robby now spends his life sharing how easy it is to ask and receive. It starts with a simple query, "What is the one thing in your past you are clinging to so deeply? What's the one thing that's holding you back?"

Letting go and then letting God take over is the path to becoming permanently unhooked. Robby reiterates, "All that is required is to ask." Undoubtedly, the number who receive help and hope from his message is far greater than Robby will ever know. The parade of cards was only a small sampling.

CHAPTER 23

HELPING OTHERS

I have found the paradox that if I love until it hurts, then there is no hurt,
but only more love.

MOTHER TERESA

Sylvia

I sobbed uncontrollably as I wrote the sordid story of my addiction. *Reliving the mistakes I made, the decisions I regret, and the wrongs I've done hurt deeply—maybe more than when I was living through them. Then, my feelings were numbed by drugs. As I wrote my saga for this book, I was stone sober—not one pill to soften the remembrances or the remorse I felt. But I wanted to tell my story—if it will help just one person and give hope when that person feels hopeless, then dredging the dirt of my life back up will have been worth the pain.*

One of the tenets of Celebrate Recovery is that a person is truly recovering when she recycles the pain in her life for others. An addict shouldn't assume that she has to be talented, articulate, or brilliant to share with others. Ordinary people are addicted, and they want to hear the voices of other ordinary people who have made the treacherous but fulfilling journey to recovery. That is why sharing is such an integral part of meetings of recovery support groups. First, hearing others lets the addict know she is not alone—that others face the same temptations she does; that others fail and have to get unhooked again. Second, giving to others is an obligation. If the addict has been given the gift of recovery, the best way to express her gratitude is to help others get and stay unhooked.

SHARING STORIES OF RECOVERY

Diane Monteleone, Program Director of Focus Healthcare of Tennessee, learned early about addiction, and it seemed the lessons just kept coming. Born to an alcoholic father, Monteleone was one of nine children. One of her brothers suffered from cocaine addiction, and she watched him lose business after business, destroying his life. Scared to death of addiction, Monteleone fought her own battle with an eating disorder. But she couldn't totally escape the lure of alcoholism, marrying a man who struggled with his dependence on liquor. Combined with a bipolar disorder that made her husband violent and aggressive, her husband's substance abuse was more than Monteleone could take, and she finally left him, taking her three children. Believing she had finally pulled away from the tentacles of alcoholism, she watched fearfully as its long reach pulled her son in after his father was shot and killed in 2000.

Some people would have caved after dealing with so many addictions, but Monteleone has not only overcome her eating disorder, she has also dedicated her life to helping others. With a smile, Monteleone concedes that many counselors are "wounded warriors," people who have been in the trenches themselves. With a degree in family counseling, her experiences give her empathy and understanding as she works with patients at Focus Healthcare of Tennessee. Although she no longer provides direct counseling herself, in her position as Program Director at Focus, she is responsible for patient care, and she avows there is nothing more rewarding than working at a facility offering hope to those hooked by addiction.

The addict's experiences give him empathy—he has felt the same pain, experienced the same hopelessness. He can identify with other addicts wherever they are in their journey. That's what made Gary A, Terry C, and Monteleone such effective counselors. For more than ten years each, they dedicated their lives to listening, caring, and helping addicts, most of whom wanted a way out of the blackness of their lives. They encouraged recovering addicts to be honest and open, to confront hurtful experiences, and to develop skills for coping with life. In his work, Gary observed that young people often act like they don't want love, but they really crave it—something he knew from his own childhood. In many ways, addicted adults are no different—they pretend they are in control and need no help, yet their actions cry out for relief and support.

Gary and Terry could also identify with addicts who had a hammer hanging over their heads. Gary notes that he found personally and in treating others that fear is a great motivator—fear of losing your family, your job, or going to jail. "If a person has consequences to face, they do better in treatment," he proclaims.

The most difficult people to help are those who are older, comfortable financially, and who don't have to worry about losing a spouse or a job. Gary's most intractable cases came from automobile assembly plants in Michigan. The union workers weren't motivated—they knew when they completed treatment, their jobs were guaranteed. And, as long as they had income, most of their wives stuck around despite multiple relapses— one person Gary counseled had been in treatment 17 times. Even though Gary couldn't personally identify with such lack of motivation, he knows addiction is a disease, so he never stopped trying, even with the stubborn cases. He's the first to admit that as soon as you label someone as not having a chance, he makes it. No one is hopeless.

If a recovering addict doesn't have the educational credentials to be a counselor, she can still use her experiences to help others. Most recovery groups ask members to have sponsors. After attending a group for a time, it is likely someone will turn to another member and say, "Will you be my sponsor?" Recovering addicts with some sobriety under their belts should not forget such a request is a plea for help, an appeal for a guiding hand. One of the most discouraging times in a recovering addict's life is to be told, "No" when she asks someone to be a sponsor. Regardless of the reason, it feels like a rejection. That's exactly what happened to Sylvia—twice. After her second request was denied, she gave up and went on with her recovery despite not having a formal relationship with a supporter. Thankfully, she made it without a sponsor to call when she felt overwhelmed with problems, partly because she had strong support within her family. Perhaps more importantly, after making countless promises to God, she intended to keep this one. Others might not be as fortunate. When asked to be someone's sponsor and cannot, a person shouldn't just say "no." Instead, the reason should be explained and assurance given that another person can be found to be their sponsor. Then, if possible, the recovering addict should help make that happen.

OTHER WAYS TO SHARE

The ways to share an addict's story are as innumerable as the person's experiences. In addition to writing a book, becoming a counselor, and being a sponsor, an addict can give his testimony in church settings, talk with co-workers, help families understand addiction, volunteer in treatment centers, become an advocate for prescription drug control, and on and on. Terry C, the Chattanooga artist whose story was told earlier, shares his life's misadventures on his gallery web page. It takes tremendous courage to put the darkest days of his life in black and white for the world to read, but he tells his story to show others that recovery is possible even for a homeless street person.

What the recovering addict says and how he says it is not as important as the fact that he is willing to share—honestly and humbly. As he articulates his story, he should think about what would have helped him when he was abusing. Clearly, a lecture was not what he wanted to hear. More likely, he wanted to hear someone say, "I was hooked, but I am now unhooked. If I can do it, you can do it. No one is hopeless."

Sylvia

As Mother Teresa said in the quote at the beginning of this chapter, I loved enough to be willing to hurt as I wrote my story for this book. And, in loving, I found my hurt lifting. I can't say it is totally gone, but knowing I may have helped others in their battle to get unhooked eases my guilt and makes my hurt less raw.

A BROKEN PIECE OF MIRROR

Sylvia has learned the same lesson Robert Fulghum conveyed about a young boy who found a broken piece of mirror on the island of Crete after Nazis wiped out whole villages as retribution for peasants who bravely attacked Nazi paratroopers with kitchen knives and hay scythes. Years later, at an institute built on the island to spread the message of human understanding and peace, that young boy, now a man, pulled the small piece of mirror, the size of a quarter, from his pocket and told his story: He was a small child during the war. One day, on the road where the Nazis attacked, he found the broken pieces of a mirror from a German motorcycle that had crashed. He kept the largest piece and became fascinated that he could reflect light into dark places—deep holes, crevices, dark closets—where the sun couldn't reach. Later, when the young boy became a man, he discerned that the game he had played with the mirror in years past was more than a child's game—it was a metaphor for what he could do with his life. In profound insight, he came to see that his life was a fragment of a mirror whose whole he had never seen. But with the small piece he had found—with the perception he had, he could reflect light—truth, understanding, and knowledge— in hidden, dark places in the hearts of other human beings. With light reflecting from his life, he might be able to change at least a fragment of the world.

And so should each recovering addict use the light he or she found to shine light into the hearts of others whose lives may still be hidden in darkness. As the old song goes, "It only takes a spark to keep a candle glowing—and soon all those around can warm up in its glowing."

CHAPTER 24

FROM HOPELESS TO HOPEFUL—FINAL THOUGHTS

*One day at a time—this is enough. Do not look back and grieve over the past
for it is gone; and do not be troubled about the future, for it has not yet come.
Live in the present, and make it so beautiful it will be worth remembering.*

ANONYMOUS

Life is a tumultuous journey of deep valleys and steep mountains.
Very few people lead charmed lives with no trouble or heartache, and
most have tumbled from the mountaintop into dark seas, caught in the
riptides of life more than once. Problems overwhelm, temptations draw
us in, and catastrophe strikes. Sometimes we pull ourselves from the
treacherous currents quickly. Other times we allow ourselves to float
aimlessly, carried by the waves of life, unable to move toward the safety
of the shoreline. For a time—long or short—recovering addicts were
hooked to a false lifeline that kept them in deep waters. They thought
they were hopeless, and then they discovered hope. The true lifeline—a
higher power—saved them for new life.

Accepting the gift of new life requires letting go of the past. It is forever
gone, and it cannot be relived. Each day of sobriety is a gift of grace, and
that is enough. And, remember that surviving the storms of our lives is
not the only goal; we should learn how to dance in the rain.

 Life will not suddenly become easy, but if recovering addicts tackle one
day at a time, they can make it through good days and bad. Still, they
want more than that—they want to make the present so beautiful it will
be worth remembering. How is that possible?

Two birds fly over the California desert—the hummingbird and the
vulture. One of them holds the key to a joyful life.

All the vulture can see is rotting meat because that's all he looks for. He thrives on that diet. But the hummingbird ignores the carcasses and the smelly flesh of dead animals. Instead, it looks for the tiny blossoms of the cactus flowers, buzzing around until it finds the colorful blooms, almost hidden from view by the rocks.

Each bird finds what it is looking for!

What are we looking for in life? Or, a more piercing question might be: What are we finding in life? For what we are finding reveals what we are looking for.

Are there hidden diamonds we will never find because we fail to look? Is there unseen goodness in people because we look for the worst in them? Is there a purpose for our lives that remains veiled from our eyes?

Each morning we awaken to face a new day. We can choose to look for flowers in nooks and crannies or bemoan the weeds in the cracks of the sidewalk. We can marvel at the fiery grandeur of a thunderstorm threatening the horizon, or we can dread the pelts of rain about to plummet our heads. We can see the heart-wrenching need of a homeless man with his out-stretched hands or silently berate him for making us face his human wretchedness.

The new day demands to be filled. Sights and sounds color our thoughts as we make our choices. To lend a helping hand or pass a stranger by. To offer a heartfelt smile or remain absorbed in our own life's demands. To be hopeful or hopeless.

If blessed with two eyes to see, we should look for the best in life. Like the hummingbird, we should look for wildflowers secreted among the rocks. We should seek splendor in the shadows of our lives.

THOUGHTS TO LIVE BY

Focus on one of these thoughts each day, and your life can change from hopeless to hopeful:

ง

Let go of yesterday; it cannot be relived,
but it does not have to shape today or tomorrow.

ง

Don't forget bad experiences; learn from them.

You don't have to be tomorrow what you are today.

Recognize that it is never too late to start again.

Accept each day as a new beginning, filled with possibilities.

Know that a better tomorrow begins today.

Know that failure is the back door to success.
Keep trying until you get it right.

Never give up; during trying times, keep trying.

Learn to go with the flow.

Accept that you cannot control other people but know that you can
control how you feel about what they say and do.

Truth never has to be untangled.

If you don't like who you are, change.

Change how you think and you'll change your life.

Moments, not years, determine our lives.

❧

Forgive those who have hurt you, not for them but for yourself.

❧

With God at your side, anything is possible.

❧

Believe in yourself—you are capable.

❧

Ask for help when needed, accept it, and be grateful for it.

❧

Put your problems in proper perspective—
don't make mountains out of molehills.

❧

Realize if you want your life to be different, you will need
to become different yourself.

❧

The end is often the beginning.

❧

Put more faith in God than in yourself.

RESOURCES

Addiction Search (*addiction topics, blog, and treatment centers*)
www.addictionsearch.com

Addiction Resource Guide (*comprehensive directory of treatment centers*)
www.addictionresourceguide.com
P.O. Box 8612
Tarrytown, NY 10591
(914) 725-5151

Adult Children of Alcoholics (*source for adults who grew up with parents who were addicted*)
www.adultchildren.org
P.O. Box 3216
Torrance, CA 90510
(310) 534-1815

Al-Anon/Alateen (*help for friends and families of addicts*)
www.al-anon.alateen.org
1600 Corporate Landing Parkway
Virginia Beach, VA 23454
(757) 563-1600

Alcoholics Anonymous (AA) (*a fellowship of men and women who share their experience, strength and hope with each other as they recover from alcoholism. No dues or fees—the only requirement is to stop drinking*)
www.alcoholics-anonymous.org
P.O. Box 459
New York, NY 10163

AllTreatment.com (*a comprehensive resource for drug treatment centers in the United States*)
www.AllTreatment.com
1000 2nd Avenue, Suite 3700
Seattle, WA 98104

Narcotics Anonymous (NA) (*the drug addiction equivalent of AA, no fees or dues—the only requirement is to stop abusing drugs*)
www.na.org
World Service Office in Los Angeles
P.O. Box 9999
Van Nuys, CA 91409
(818) 700-9999

SAMHSA Substance Abuse Treatment Facility Locator *(searchable directory lists locations of alcohol and drug abuse facilities in the United States and includes more than 12,000 residential centers, inpatient treatment programs, and outpatient treatment programs)*
www.findtreatment.samhsa.gov

U.S. Drug Enforcement Administration (DEA) Division of Diversion Control *(division that works to identify and eliminate illicit pharmacy activities and illegal purchase of drugs online)*
www.deadiversion.usdoj.gov
Attn: Liaison and Policy Section
Washington, DC 20537

SOURCES

Anton, Leonora LaPeter. *St. Petersburg Times.* May 19, 2010.

Associated Press. "Feds hold summit on prescription drugs." *Chattanooga Times Free Press,* March 3, 2011.

Baker, John. *Life's Healing Choices.* New York: Howard Books, 2007.

Breckenridge, Megan. "Feds Crack Down on Illicit Prescription Drug Sales." http://www.sullolaw.com/Article/FedsCrackDown.html Accessed February 16, 2011.

Canfield, Clark. "The Story Behind the Tugboat Pictures." *Professional Mariner.* June/July, 2002.

[Authors' Note: The tugboat tale is a true story that was originally told in a series of photographs snapped in 1979 by someone on the drawbridge. Although published by a small newspaper at the time, the photographs did not capture much public attention until they became an Internet sensation in 2002.]

Carter, Les. *The Anger Trap: Free Yourself from Frustrations that Sabotage Your Life.* San Francisco: Jossey Bass, 2003.

Childress, Anna Rose, Ph.D. "What Is Relapse?" Home Box Office. http://www.hbo.com/addiction/15_relapse.html Retrieved January 12, 2011.

"Co-Dependency." http:///www.mentalhealthamerica.net/go/codependency Accessed January 21, 2011.

"Co-Dependency – The Problem." http://www.allaboutlifechallenges.org/codependency.htm Accessed January 21, 2011.

Collins, Judy. *Singing Lessons: A Memoir of Love, Loss, Hope, and Healing.* New York: Simon and Schuster, 1998.

Collins, Thomas R. "Invasion of the Pill Mills in South Florida." *Time,* April 13, 2010 http://www.time.com/time/nation/article. 08599.1981582.00.html Accessed January 13, 2011.

Colvin, Rod. *Prescription Drug Addiction: The Hidden Epidemic: A Guide to Understanding and Coping.* (Second Edition) Omaha, Nebraska: Addicus Books, 2002.

Colvin, Rod. *Overcoming Prescription Drug Abuse: A Guide to Understanding and Coping.* (Third Edition) Omaha, Nebraska: Addicus Books, 2008.

Conger, J. A. and Associates. *Spirit at Work: Discovering the Spirituality in Leadership.* San Francisco, California: Jossey-Bass, 1994.

Dao, James. "Powerful drug cocktails fatal for some troops." *Chattanooga Times Free Press.* February 13, 2011.

Eisley, Loren. "The Star Thrower." *The Unexpected Universe*. Orlando, Florida: Mariner Books, 1969.

"Enabling and co-dependency." http://www.allaboutlifechallenges.org/enabling-and-codependency-faq.htm Accessed January 21, 2011.

"Florida's fight against pill mills won't be helped by a needless special prosecutor." *Palm Beach Post*. January 7, 2011.

Frankl, Viktor. *Man's Search for Meaning*. Boston: Beacon Press, 1959.

Friedman, Emily. "Feds Raid Pain Clinics Suspected of Illegally Distributing Millions of Prescription Drugs." *ABC News*, March 8, 2010.

Fulghum, Robert. *It Was On Fire When I Laid Down on It*. New York: Villard Books, a Division of Random House, 1993.

Gordon, Susan Merle, Ph.D. "Relapse & Recovery: Behavioral Strategies for Change. Caron Foundation. http://alcoholism.ablut.com/cs/relapse/a/blcaron030804.htm?p=1 Accessed 1/12/2011.

Gorski, Gordon T. in Colvin, Rod. *Overcoming Prescription Drug Abuse: A Guide to Understanding and Coping*. (Third Edition) Omaha, Nebraska: Addicus Books, 2008.

Hoppe, Sherry Lee. *Faces of Grief*. Nashville, Tennessee: Wakestone Press, 2011.

Hoppe, Sherry L. "Spirituality and Higher Education Leadership." In Bruce W. Speck and Sherry L. Hoppe (eds.), *Searching for Spirituality in Higher Education*. New York: Peter Lang, 2007.

Hoppe, Sherry L. "Spirituality and Leadership." In Sherry L. Hoppe and Bruce W. Speck (eds.) , *Spirituality in Higher Education*. San Francisco, California: Jossey-Bass, 2005.

http://www.abcnews.go.com/US/story?id=7041036&page=1 Accessed March 9, 2009.

http://www.findtreatment.samhsa.gov/ Accessed January 15, 2011.

http://www.g8stories.blogspot.com/2006/11/commitment.html Accessed February 19, 2011. (Beggar story)

http://www.justice.gov/ndic/pubs11/18862/transport.htm Accessed January 24, 2011.

http://www.loosecannonartandevents.com/page/about Accessed January 31, 2011.

http://www.msnbc.msn.com/id/31707246/ns/health-addictions. Accessed July 30, 2010.

http://www.oas.samhsa.gov/nhsda.htm Accessed January 7, 2011.

http://www.sciencedaily.com/releases/2007/03/070302082810.htm Accessed January 6, 2011.

Karpman, Stephen. http://www.karpmandramatriangle.com. Accessed January 10, 2011.

Lukachick, Joy. "Doctor charged with illegally doling out pain pills." *Chattanooga Times Free Press*. March 2, 2011.

Lukachick, Joy. "Georgia pill mills on rise." *Chattanooga Times Free Press*. March 8, 2011.

Lukachick, Joy. "Pain management clinic shut down." *Chattanooga Times Free Press*. March 18, 2011.

Lukachick, Joy. "Reopening of raided clinics irks neighbors." *Chattanooga Times Free Press*. April 8, 2011.

Lutzer, Erwin W. *How to Say NO to a Stubborn Habit—even when you want to say YES*. Wheaton, Illinois: Victor Books, 1984.

McKay, Matthew and Patrick Fanning. *Prisoners of Beliefs*. Oakland, California: New Harbinger Publications, 1991.

MacDonald, Gordon. *Rebuilding Your Broken World*. Nashville, Tennessee: Thomas Nelson Publishers, 1990.

Manning, Brennan. *The Ragamuffin Gospel*. Sisters, Oregon: Multnomah Publishers, Inc., 2000.

Melemis, Steven M., Ph.D., M.D. *I Want to Change My Life*. Toronto, Ontario: Modern Therapies, 2010.

Mogil, Cindy K. *Swallowing a Bitter Pill*. Far Hills, New Jersey: New Horizon Press, 2001.

Mohney, Nell. "Life's about making music with what's left over." *Chattanooga Times Free Press,* February 19, 2011.

Monteleone, Diane. (MAFT, NCC, LAMFT, LAPC) Interview at Focus Healthcare of Tennessee, March 17, 2011.

Mooney, Michael. *Broward Palm Beach Times*. March 18, 2010. Accessed January 14, 2011. http://blogs.browardpalmbeach.com/juice/2010/03/kentucky_police_struggle_pain_pill_pipeline.php.

Nakken, Craig. *Reclaim Your Family from Addiction*. Center City, Minnesota: Hazelden, 2000.

Napper, Robert. "Pain clinics challenge Florida's pill mill bill in federal court."

Florida Independent http://floridaindependent.com/9273/ Accessed January 13, 2010.

Narcotics Anonymous. Chatsworth, California: Narcotics Anonymous World Services, Inc., 2008.

Nelson, Bryce. "The Addictive Personality: Common Traits Are Found." *New York Times.* January 18, 1983.

Palmer, Parker J. *A Hidden Wholeness.* San Francisco, California: Jossey-Bass, 2004.

"Patterns and Characteristics of Codependence." http://www.coda.org/tools4recovery/patterns-new.htm Accessed January 21, 2011.

Potter-Efron, Ronald T. *Rage: A Step-by-Step Guide to Overcoming Explosive Anger.* Oakland, California: New Harbinger Publications, 2007.

Ruden, Ronald A. with Byalick, Marcia. *The Craving Brain.* New York: Harper Collins, 2003.

Seligman, Martin E. P. *Learned Optimism.* New York: Pocket Books, 1990.

St. John, Bonnie. *Live Your Joy.* New York: Faithwords, Hatchette Book Group, 2009.

Sulfridge, Adam S. "Five more arrested in 'pill pipeline.'" *Times Tribune,* January 22, 2010.

Unknown Author. Story of carrots, eggs, and coffee beans. http://oboerista.wordpress.com/2007/08/22/carrot-egg-coffee-a-life-lesson-from-the-kitchen/ Accessed February 20, 2011.

Unknown Source. "Shaking It Off and Stepping It Up."

Untitled Handout. Focus Healthcare of Tennessee, An Alcohol and Drug Abuse Treatment Center, 2010.

Vela, Jose Julio. "Getting Sober: Feds Attempt to Crack Down on Internet Drug Pushers." http://www.law.uh.edu/healthlaw/perspectives/2010/(JV)%20Internet.pdf Accessed February 16, 2011.

Waitley, Denis. *Seeds of Greatness.* Old Tappan, New Jersey: Fleming H. Revell Company, 1983.

Washton, Arnold, and Donna Boundy. *Willpower's Not Enough: Recovering from Addictions of Every Kind.* New York: Harper & Rowe Publishers, 1989.

COPYRIGHT PERMISSIONS

The authors are grateful for permission to include the following previously copyrighted material:

Quote from *Prisoners of Beliefs*. McKay, Matthew and Patrick Fanning (1991).
Reprinted by permission of New Harbinger Publications, Oakland, California.

Twelve Steps and other excerpts from *Narcotics Anonymous*. (2008).
Reprinted by permission of NA World Services, Inc. All rights reserved.

Quote from *Willpower's Not Enough*. Arnold Washton and Donna Boundy (1989).
Reprinted with permission of HarperCollins Publishers.

Quote from *Overcoming Prescription Drug Addiction*. Rod Colvin (2008).
Reprinted with permission of Addicus Books.

Quotes from *Life's Healing Choices*. John Baker.
Reprinted with permission of Howard Books.

Excerpt from *"Patterns and Characteristics of Codependence."*
http://www.coda.org/tools4recovery/patterns-new.htm.
Reprinted with permission of Council on Co-Dependents Anonymous.

Quotes from *Singing Lessons: A Memoir of Love, Loss, Hope, and Healing*. Joan Collins (1998).
Reprinted with permission of Simon and Schuster.

Quotes from *Ragamuffin Gospel*. Brennan Manning (2000).
Reprinted with permission of Multnomah Publishers.

A MATTER OF CONSCIENCE, Redemption of a hometown hero, Bobby Hoppe. *With Dennie B. Burke.*

SIPS OF SUSTENANCE, Grieving the Loss of Your Spouse.

FACES OF GRIEF, Stories of Surviving Sorrow and Finding Hope

Made in the USA
Lexington, KY
05 October 2012